T0290512

Problem
Finding and
Problem
Solving

Problem Finding and Problem Solving

Alfred W.W. Schoennauer

Nelson-Hall nh Chicago

To my wife, Nelda
and
my children, Mark, Cheryl, Sandra, and Debra

LIBRARY OF CONGRESS CATALOGING IN PUBLICATION DATA

Schoennauer, Alfred W. W.
  Problem finding and problem solving.

  Includes index.
  1. Problem solving. 2. Management.   I. Title.
HD30.29.S54   658.4'03   81–9591
ISBN 0–88229–590–X (cloth)   AACR2
ISBN 0–88229–792–9 (paper)

Copyright © 1981 by Alfred W. W. Schoennauer

Manufactured in the United States of America

10 9 8 7 6 5 4 3 2 1

Contents

Preface

Problems can only be solved after they have been identified, but the temptation to proceed against symptoms rather than causes appears as an ever-present phenomenon in organizations. In addition, managers differ in their ability to find problems—and to solve them. A unique set of skills seems to be required for each area, and few managers are really proficient in both. Usually it is problem finding that is slighted, and so a high probability exists that the problem-solving focus becomes misdirected.

This book is a manual, a short course, in the techniques and methods of problem finding and of problem solving. A review is also provided in general management methods, in leadership styles, of information and resource requirements for identifying and solving problems or for implementing and evaluating courses of action.

Some of the premises upon which this book is based should be made explicit. The first is that most organization problems are caused by faulty decisions of managers. This, in turn, is based on the idea that managers and their decisions are the catalyst that makes organizations function. If things go wrong, managers are then held accountable. This is not to say that managers are morally accountable for the misconduct of their subordinates, but rather that, unless managers recognize that this is the "way of organizational life," they will soon find to their regret that ten aspirants to their job are waiting in the shadows for a chance to improve upon the incumbent's efforts.

The second premise is that management methods and techniques are situational. This is not to suggest a situational ethics concept, since the methods, with some exceptions, are neutral tools. Their efficacy lies in using them in the right situation.

The methodology employed in this book distinguishes management systems from operations, problem finding from problem solving, after-the-fact problem finding from before-the-fact problem finding. It provides the means for rigorously considering multiple perspectives of a course of action and the means for vigorously justifying a proposed solution. The book also shows ways to consider the interrelationships of factors that abound in most situations. It is a heuristics approach.

The ideas expressed here have application to organizations in general. The book should prove to be a helpful checklist for the capable manager in today's increasingly complex life. It should serve as a valuable training device for the aspiring practitioner of the art of managing an organization or some subdivision of an organization.

Chapter 1 sets the perspective of problem finding and solving. Chapter 2 deals at length with problem finding after the organization has experienced unsatisfactory performance. Chapter 3 extends the problem-finding analysis into the management system that produced an inappropriate decision. This is necessary so that any deficiency that may exist in the decision-making system itself can be recognized and attempts can be made to correct it, so as to reduce a recurrence of inappropriate decisions. Chapter 4 analyzes problem finding before any unsatisfactory results have occurred. This is preventive management, the most difficult, but offering the greatest rewards. Chapter 5 recommends a problem-solving thought process or methodology. Chapter 6 applies these concepts to an actual business situation. In that situation, an organization was experiencing serious cost increases that theoretically should not have been occurring. The case provides an interesting application of many of the aspects of problem finding and solving process.

This book represents over a decade of curiosity, research, and experiment in problem finding and solving. The methodology has been used in seminars in business case analysis courses at three universities separated by twelve thousand miles, at both the graduate and undergraduate level. A great deal has already been said about the "policy" course as the integrative mechanism, the top-management perspective, the capstone course, the interdisciplinary course, etc. The perspectives and interest of "policy" faculty, however, often differ, and, too often, the frustration of both students and faculty is the result. A great deal of apprehension and uneasiness is a normal reaction pattern. However, seminar participants have repeatedly reacted positively to a preplanned analytical process. The discipline of a methodology has been one of the features of the course that they most appreciated, for it represents a tangible tool they can take with them into the outside world.

1
Introduction to Problem Finding and Problem Solving

Introduction
The Symptoms Approach
The Leadership Approach
The Technology Approach
The Information Approach
The People Approach
The Dollar Approach
The Materiel Approach
The Governance Approach
The Environmental Approach
Some Explanations for the Inappropriate Uses of
     Problem-Finding Approaches
  The manager's environment
  Corporate and personal capabilities
  Forces within the manager
Some Key Definitions
Some Basic Problem-Finding and Problem-Solving Premises
    and Guidelines
  Problem finding and problem solving involve unique situations
    that call for unique capabilities
  Management errors are the most common causes of undesirable
    results
  Management is the means, the catalyst, for moving the
    organization into action and for getting desired results
  The content of a decision is largely determined by the situation
  For every action there is a reaction

1

Introduction

Problems are characteristic of all organized activity. The chief executive officer of a medium-sized corporation recently ventured to say that everything seems to be a problem in today's world.

A survey of corporate annual reports reveals the kinds of problems often facing corporations:

- Depressed economic conditions
- Cost increases
- Increase in foreign currency values vis-à-vis the dollar
- Unanticipated capital expenditures
- Slower than expected growth rate
- Corporate price increases cut into sales volume
- Bad weather
- Foreign competition
- Consumer resistance, trading down
- Higher interest rates
- Loss of plant due to fire
- Natural gas shortage
- Reduced market value of land

Other problems not always publicly admitted also exist. The range of problems is practically unlimited. Small companies may list money as their most important problem. The growing company seeks space or finds itself unable to keep the increased scope of its operations under control. Mature organizations face plant and equipment obsolescence. Market and product change is a constant problem. Superiors point at the ineptness of their subordinates. Subordinates would like to see their bosses change. Line superiors keenly feel their lack of authority. They resent the abuse of clear policy by many of the corporate officers. Pressure from all sides is a continuing irritation.

How do managers deal with such problems? Identifying the problem is a necessary first step, but experience has shown that it is extremely difficult to secure a consensus as to what the "real" problem is. And what many identify as problems constitute nothing more than a symptoms list. Many decades ago Elton Mayo, reflecting upon the Western Electric Company studies, commented that the reactions of employees fail to give any positive clue as to what the real sources of employee irritation may be (Mayo). The sources, the causes, are—or should be—the subjects of interest to managers. Unfortunately, the aspirin approach, submerging and soothing the symptoms, still appears to be one of the most popular methods of "problem solving."

This book is an attempt to provide a stepwise process— i.e., to give some structure to problem-finding and problem-solving activities. It seeks to create a perspective that will slice through a symptoms list, identify clues, and aid in isolating them from their causes. Here is an approach that should aid in identfying an "excuse" for poor performance as an excuse. It should assist and encourage thinking in depth at both the problem-identification and the problem-solving stages. Illogical reasoning should be more readily identifiable, and rhetoric without content can be shown for the facade it is. The findings of behavioral and organizational research, as well as relationships that may have been observed by practitioners, should readily fit into the structure and so become part of the logic in problem identification and problem solving.

A meaningful by-product of the problem-finding and problem-solving methodology is that it provides the perspective for identifying and evaluating some of the approaches to problem finding that are being utilized by organizations.

The Symptoms Approach

First, the symptoms approach. The term *symptom* is just another way of referring to the effect of some causal element. Undesirable symptoms may include such things as the failure to make an ample profit margin, loss of sales, or low morale. The position held by those who use this approach seems to be one that says, "Don't attempt to interfere, that would only make things worse. Keep the status quo." They are really saying, "This is the nature of the thing." In effect they imply that the cause lies in the inherent nature of the person, the equipment, or the situation. Short of retiring the resource, hands off. In scientific jargon, the nature of the resource or the nature of the situational factors is seen as the causal element for random variations in performance. No action is called for. The problem is viewed as short run. If the discomfort becomes acute, look away or take a sedative. Tomorrow will be different.

The approach has elements of truth. Few work at the same pace, have constant output, each month, each week, each day, or, for that matter, each hour. A piece of sophisticated milling equipment, for example, may produce output of slightly varying dimensions. It is probably designed to produce within a designated tolerance range. Variations within this range are random occurrences. No action is called for, nor will such action be successful if the intent is to narrow the range of output. If the output at the extreme ends of the range is not marketable, then one must secure another piece of equipment that is capable of producing within a more acceptable range. However, when output is characterized as the result of randomness—i.e., the inherent nature of the resource or the environment—but in reality some new factor has entered the situation, then the symptoms approach is inappropriate.

The symptoms approach is a popular one. It would seem to reflect understanding and tolerance, but it can be used to avoid potentially threatening situations. When sales are down, the excuse of randomness may hide mismanagement or delay the unpleasantness of disciplining the crew, tightening up on procedures, exercising control, or redirecting the organization.

The key to distinguishing between a random occurrence and one that has assignable causes—i.e., one caused by nonrandom factors—lies initially in knowing the capabilities of the resources or the random behaviors of environmental variables. Both resources and environment have random and non-random characteristics, but it is the nonrandom element that is important in problem finding. For example, salesman Thomas misses his quota by 10 percent. He also was passed over for promotion several weeks ago. Here it would be fair to assume that the drop in output was caused by a nonrandom, assignable factor—namely, the decision not to promote salesman Thomas.

The Leadership Approach

The leadership approach tends to assign blame for undesirable results upon an inadequate or inappropriate leadership style. A subset of this approach sees the breakdown of communications or their inadequacy as the cause for poor performance. The term *supervision* could be substituted, but generally that term is reserved for the role of the foreman and those who hold similar positions in the hierarchy.

Leadership and communications are critical managerial functions. They occur in all organized activity. They are pervasive. They permeate the whole of the unit or department. Many leadership styles and hybrids have been identified and associated with either success or failure. These styles are deeply imbedded in the personality of the individual and thus are difficult to change.

Unfortunately, there is a tendency to make leadership and communications the scapegoats. Often, if not usually, they may need improvement, but that process is long, painful, expensive, and subject to ethical and moral dimensions. This is particularly true if an attempt is made to get at some of the more deeply entrenched causes for poor communications and leadership. The results, too, are highly probabilistic. Other causal elements may be present and more amenable to correction. This is not to say that some of the techniques for improving communications and leadership should not be tried. They have proven their value to organizations. Learning the obstacles to effective communication may make one more sensitive to one's own style, particularly if this is carried out under the direction and understanding counsel of an able administrator or coach.

The Technology Approach

The technology approach places the onus for poor performance upon technology—that is, the lack or the improper application of the technical know-how for running an operation. It takes a good engineer to design a sound structure, medical proficiency to treat patients, teaching skills to train students, financial acumen to tend to the monetary requirements of an organization, a technical manufacturing base to produce automobiles, manufacture cement, extract minerals from water, or make new products.

Many small companies experience phenomenal successes solely by virtue of their technical skills but suffer a dramatic reversal as they expand their operations. They probably failed to develop an appreciation of the role of management, particularly the structural dimensions. After this dramatic experience, new managerial elements are injected, but they may become overemphasized. With the blossoming and growth of the bureaucratic structure, with its attendant inflexibilities, the infusion of updated technology may be circumvented by the maze of red tape. And so the typical birth-growth-fade cycle may be repeated, this time due to the lack of technology update.

Technology is obviously a variable critical to success, but it is not a guarantee of success. Equipment may represent the most recent technological knowledge, but its application may be limited or its successes largely unproven. Instances exist in industry today in which expensive and modern equipment was purchased only to be used at a fraction of its capabilities. As the technologically poor country may have more urgent needs than an infusion of modern know-how, so the organization may have needs that have a higher priority than technology inputs. However, at some stage the introduction of new

technology in terms of product, service, or processes must
have top priority.

The Information Approach

The information approach views unsatisfactory results as
emanating from a lack of information. Such claims often
have substantial validity. Sales must know the nature of consumer demand, production must know what lines to produce,
inventory control must inform purchasing when the reorder
point is reached, management must learn of industry and
competitor actions. Here information becomes the lifeblood
of management decision making.

The need for information and the need for effective communications must be distinguished. A communications breakdown (discussed under the leadership approach) occurs in
the sending-receiving process. The information was available,
and it was intended to be transmitted, but somewhere in the
sending-receiving process obstacles arose to hinder effective
communication. In contrast, the information approach assumes either that the information was unavailable and therefore could not be provided, or that it was available but deliberately or through ignorance withheld. The warehousing or
suppression of information at the grass-roots level is a common phenomenon. The propensity to discolor facts in suc-
cessive levels in the hierarchy is an ever-present human
frailty. The movement of needed information upward, down-
ward, or crosswise, as well as the availability of relevant
environmental data, represent important dimensions of the
information problem.

On the other hand, Russell L. Ackoff, writing in *Management Science,* has suggested that an information problem
may arise because—

- Most managers do not lack relevant information but
rather suffer from an overload of irrelevant data.
- Most managers do not know what information they need
so they want everything to play it safe.

- Most managers do not know how to use relevant information.
- More information does not necessarily mean better performance (Ackoff).

The problems suggested here may call for a radical redesign of the management information system itself, with emphasis on determining just what information is needed by each decision center.

The People Approach

Under the people approach to problem finding, the blame for undesirable results is placed upon the shoulders of the human resource, the employees, and usually the rank and file are chosen for this distinction. The problem is the kind of candidates personnel sends down to us. It is the skill level of the workers. Their attitude and values fail to mesh with company purpose. They fail to respond. They live for the weekend. Their big concerns are security and money; yet they fail to give a fair day's effort. Any attempt to gain their cooperation, get them integrated into the work group, or to give them the opportunity to learn something new meets with disinterest and resistance.

Perhaps an inherent perversity of man may be reflected in these observations, but these attitudes cannot be attributed solely to the rank and file. Wrongheadedness is not their monopoly. Managers often have few bouquets to distribute to their own ranks in the hierarchy. The point is that, from the perspectives of both the workers and the managers, this approach singles out people as the culprits, but rarely are situations that simple. Accusing employees of being the cause of poor performance could be used by some as a smoke screen to obscure other manifest failures. Nevertheless, people inadequacies in some instances are real. In other situations, such conditions may have been brought about by the management practices themselves. Whether or not people ought to react so negatively is not the issue here. Rather, in today's world managers are, in effect, evaluated on the basis of the cooperation they receive and on the basis of the skills they can develop in the people under their jurisdiction.

The Dollar Approach

The dollar approach views unsatisfactory results from the perspective of too little money, too late. In our capitalistic economy, money obviously is an absolute prerequisite. After the symptoms approach, this is probably the next-most-popular problem-finding route. Incontrovertible evidence continues to abound, however, that a sizable portion of bankruptcies, particularly among the small and the newer business ventures, is caused, not by the lack of funds, but by an inexcusable ignorance of where the business stands financially. Improper records, or simply the lack of adequate records, is the initial offense; the inability to analyze and interpret these data is the second major offense. Partially as a result of these conditions, funds that had been available were not put to best use or evaporated through poor cash control procedures.

The Materiel Approach

The materiel approach focuses on equipment, machinery, plant, plant location, raw materials, tools, or supplies. It finds these to be the primary sources of poor performance. Without a doubt, the physical tools and resources do make a difference. Without the weapons, the battle was lost. Yet history has shown that inferior weaponry coupled with determination may overcome the materiel superiority of others. The same commentary can be applied to industry, schools, or hospitals, but in these instances managerial skills replace determination as the prime mover.

The Governance Approach

Another route to problem finding is the governance approach. Deviations in performance are viewed, under this approach, as ultimately caused by the inappropriate decisions of managers. If it is the managers who plan, organize, control, make the decisions that govern activity, then, when things do go wrong, it must be the management decisions that are responsible.

The governance approach also identifies extraorganizational factors that may influence behavior as heavily as formal decisions do. These factors may include personal goals of employees or group norms, all of which can run counter to the directives of management. When an employee behaves in a way that is conducive to his or her welfare but counterproductive for the organization, then the extraorganizational influences become an obstacle to organizational success. For example, empire building, political alliances, and pilferages are behaviors that are directed to the enhancement, the security, or other goals of individuals or groups. Such behaviors, incidentally, are often condoned, encouraged, or even ignored by management, thus putting the onus once again on managerial deficiencies.

The Environmental Approach

The environmental approach points to external occurrences as the cause for unsatisfactory results. Competitor practices, taxes, economic conditions, inflation, unions, zoning ordinances, environmentalists, and the like are seen as responsible for organizational problems. This approach has some validity; nevertheless, in most cases, it either betrays unimaginative management or simply reflects an inability to manage effectively.

Generally a response to environmental opportunity or constraints fits a typical reaction triad: attack, retreat, or join forces. The join or retreat reactions simply reflect the environmental conditions. The attack strategy, however, seeks to influence environmental change or profit from it, through lobbying, advertising, public relations work, beating the competition, new product development activity, or introducing new equipment to neutralize a sharp rise in labor costs. It views opportunities as events to grasp and constraints as temporary obstacles.

In contrast, the join and retreat options view environmental occurrences as insurmountable obstacles or as opportunities beyond their singular grasp. The join strategy simply reflects acceptance or followership as an appropriate response. Price followership is a typical reaction to price change. Competitive styles are copied. Mergers become viable options.

The retreat strategy is defensive in character. It is typical of declining industries as well as mature companies that are slowly fading due in part to their failure to maintain an offensive posture with respect to their environment. The retreat strategy is reflected by decisions to reduce the scope of operations or by the phenomena experienced in a broad spectrum of U.S. industry soon after World War II when companies responded unduly to union demands as they sought to avoid a delay in sharing in the backlog of pent-up consumer and industrial demand. Both the join and the retreat strategies reflect a management approach to problem finding that blames environmental circumstances as causes for poor performance.

Some Explanations for the Inappropriate Uses of Problem-Finding Approaches

It is possible, albeit speculative, to point out some of the factors that push, pull, direct, or influence a manager to take or be forced to take a certain position with respect to problem finding. While all approaches have valid applications, one may wonder why so many invalid applications are made. Some understanding, perhaps, can be gained by assessing the environment in which managers must carry out their work, by assessing their personal capabilities and the organization resources at their disposal, or by looking at some of the forces within themselves that may influence them one way or another.

The Manager's Environment

It is to be expected that a manager's primary interest lies with the department, unit, or job for which he or she is held accountable. Despite promptings from superiors, training seminars, threats, or reprisals, most managers continue to see the world from the perspective of their own job.

The formal criteria upon which the manager will be evaluated obviously play an important role in setting options. When the criteria are in conflict with some of the desires of a manager's superiors, the resulting frustration and vacillation are understandable. When a manager's immediate superior is under pressure, the pressure is passed down the line. Immediate action may be demanded, forcing a short-run perspective and the short-circuiting of an orderly problem-search process. Avenues that should be explored may be closed. What is expedient for the moment becomes the way to go.

Corporate and Personal Capabilities

Resources to facilitate the problem-finding process may limit effectiveness. Information is seldom complete; the relevant and irrelevant are not sorted for the manager. Time may be short; the budget, tight. The manager's personal repertoire of perceptual, emotional, physical, and intellectual capabilities is also limited. This means he or she may fail to see what should have been seen, may observe and interpret as relevant what, in fact, is irrelevant. A person may fear to err or to swim against opposition.

Important skill and attitudinal areas surface in problem finding. Among them are social sensitivity, technical sensitivity, and listening skills. Social sensitivity comes into play in observing and interpreting events; in distinguishing fact from feeling; in detecting relationships among happenings, activities, and participants; in sorting the relevant from the irrelevant; in reducing the many variables of a situation into a limited list of crucial variables; in taking tentative positions while in the problem-identification process in order to remain receptive to new discoveries and new relationships.

Among the more important technical skills are the capabilities for understanding financial data and financial ratios and their relevance and meaning to problem identification. Data on cost accounting, inventory control, logistics costs and marketing comprise some of the more important quantitative areas in which the problem finders must enmesh themselves.

Listening skills are one of the most important ways for sizing up a situation, but such skills often become a fading art when a manager rises in the hierarchy and becomes more accustomed to speak than to listen.

Ralph Nichols has observed that listening by men in authority is rare. By virtue of their position, many of them make only a superficial effort: their concerns tend toward mannerism, tone, posture, choice of words, and the way in which subordinates express themselves. He suggests that managers should attempt to listen for the gist of the message rather than to gather innumerable little facts; should concentrate on the message content and ignore the vehicle being used; should avoid submitting to emotional words that interrupt real listening; and should avoid the tendency to evade those ideas that cannot immediately be reconciled in their minds inasmuch as the real message may then be lost (Nichols).

The attainment of the social skills, in particular, is partially dependent upon an appreciation of the complexities of organization behavior and upon a spirit of humility that recognizes the innate limitations of any one person. On the other hand, the successful application of these skills, once acquired, depends upon self-confidence that is based on reality rather than on fiction. Acquiring this precarious mix of humility and confidence is a difficult achievement and maintaining it is equally difficult.

Forces within the Manager

The forces of influence within a manager often play a major role in determining the problem-finding path that a person will or can take. Influences may come in the form of personal goals, aspirations, temperament, needs, and desires. One tends to view a situation in terms of one's most pressing and unfilled needs. Attitudes toward risk, people, authority, and work, underlying personal values, and beliefs as to cause-effect relationships may further serve as sources of influence.

The interplay of external and internal influences may lead to ineffectiveness partially as a result of the problem finder's behavior—for example, (1) a defensive posture in order to protect self or others, (2) a habitual behavioral pattern or one that has proven successful on some previous occasion, (3) a reflection of some important unfilled need, (4) a preconceived assessment of the situation, (5) a reflection of powerful external pressures that overwhelm other considerations, (6) an approach peculiar to the individual's style and capabilities, or (7) an imitation of some respected idol.

Other ramifications could be itemized. Impatience and arrogance may push one to seek solutions before the problem is defined. One may assume the problem has been identified when in fact what displeases has been identified. Or repeated failures in problem finding may lead to a cynical attitude, particularly when the unpredictable nature of the human variable is added.

One kind of difficulty in the problem-finding process is emphasized by Van de Ven and others, who point out that, if the manager is a factor in a problem situation, he or she becomes anxious about the kind of solution that will evolve, and so problem solving develops a stronger pull than problem finding. In addition, the personally involved manager tends to focus on problem areas outside his or her responsibility (Van de Ven and Delbecq). And so, it seems that conventional and socially acceptable problem areas become the only ones that are explored.

Some Key Definitions

The purpose of a problem-finding process is to establish the need for change. It is directed to finding the causes for unsatisfactory performance. The causes become the problem.

This implies that the "real" problem is not results, but rather that which brought about the results. Problem finding therefore is not simply finding some cause, but must involve a probing process, within the allowable range of freedom that the situation may allow, in order to uncover the most basic causes that are within the power of the manager to treat or control. According to this perspective, simply identifying resources (people, information, technology, money, or matériel) is probably insufficient. A further inquiry must be made: i.e., Why were inappropriate resources provided or allowed? Why did management respond in this way? Most unsatisfactory results are probably caused by management fumbles, and so inappropriate decisions must be identified, and the decision-making system that produced the inappropriate decision must, in turn, be analyzed to determine, Why did management make that decision?

Problem solving, on the other hand, is in essence decision making. Problem solving has several applications: first, at an initial stage of designing an organization or a new project; second, at the redesign stage when some aspect of the management of the organization has been found deficient by the problem-finding inquiry.

Some Basic Problem-Finding and Problem-Solving Premises and Guidelines

Unique Situations Call for Unique Capabilities

Problem finding deals with recapturing the elusive past, evaluating the bits and pieces, uncovering what transpired and what the significant causal factors may be. Problem solving, on the other hand, deals with possible future consequences of a course of action. Problem-finding capability is that of a sleuth, discovering and piecing together past events; problem solving anticipates the consequences and implications of a contemplated course of action.

In subsequent sections, problem finding will be divided into after-the-fact situations and before-the-fact situations. The former deal with problem identification after unsatisfactory results have occurred. Before-the-fact analysis, however, deals with finding potential causes before unsatisfactory results can occur.

Management Errors Are the Most Common Causes of Undesirable Results

The great preponderance of undesirable results can be traced directly or indirectly to management fumbles. This implies that the decisions of management are the major forces that lead to ineffectiveness or inefficiency. The implications are both frightening and reassuring—frightening in the sense that this responsibility usually rests with a small minority— the managers—yet reassuring in the sense that management skills can be taught, acquired, or improved upon through the formal learning process and/or on-the-job experience. When management responsibilities and power are decentralized through delegation and participative methods, the dire implications may be somewhat diminished. However, such decentralization can have serious costs, particularly with respect to determining who is to be held accountable as well as having to train more and more employees in managerial skills. Chapter 2 will suggest some guidelines as to an appropriate mix of autocratic and democratic approaches to decision making.

Management Is the Catalyst

Management is the means, the catalyst, for moving the organization into action and for getting desired results. Management is the governance mechanism, the prime source of influence. Management provides the overall objectives and strategies for directing the efforts of its employees toward a predetermined goal. These basic decisions are particularized and redefined through the hierarchial levels and into the ranks themselves through innumerable tactical and control procedures.

A Decision Is Determined by the Situation

The content of a specific decision is largely determined by the situation. Situational management implies that there are few management techniques appropriate to all conditions and circumstances. For example, a decision to decentralize authority may be appropriate for some situations but inappropriate in others; carefully defined job descriptions may be necessary for some companies but unnecessary for others; or precise procedures and methods may be an absolute necessity in some operations but too restrictive in others. Empirical research has identified some of the factors that distinguish situations: (1) size, number, and scope of markets, products, resources, or activity; (2) the nature of the activity—routine or nonroutine; (3) the nature of the resource utilized—predictable-unpredictable; stable-unstable, uniform-nonuniform; (4) the nature of the underlying technology—certain-uncertain, rapid-slow change; (5) the nature of the environment—certain-uncertain, stable-dynamic, uniform-diverse, rapid-slow change; (6) the time period—short run–long run; and (7) the nature of the organization's goals—simple or complex (Perrow).

For Every Action There Is a Reaction

In management terminology this means that every decision has its costs and benefits. General Motors President Alfred Sloan sent his team back to the drawing board when it could not discover any disadvantage to a proposed course of action. A short time later, after some thought, the proposal was soundly defeated. The point is that both costs and benefits must be recognized in order that a "good" decision can be made.

Management Responsibilities Deal with Two Entities

Management responsibilities deal with two entities: the management of the organization's external environment and the administration of its internal functions. Management's external and internal responsibilities are usually carried out by a type of specialization: an organization will usually attempt to isolate its environment-related tasks from its internal operations. For example, purchasing is performed by a separate department rather than by those who use the materials; industrial relations are the specific responsibility of an industrial relations department rather than of each unit employing workers. This type of specialization is intended to protect the internal operations of an organization from direct intrusions of external forces. It also serves as a means for controlling or routinizing the impact of environmental forces. Of course, the economics of specialization is also a significant factor. In some instances, however, this kind of specialization may not be appropriate. Chapter 2 will deal extensively with the situational characteristics of organization structure.

Problem Finding Must Identify Causes

Problem finding must ultimately identify causes that are within the discretionary control of the level of management that must correct the situation. It would be quite useless for the production superintendent to merely suggest that it is the attitude of the president toward the union that is the cause of production's high cost profile. The superintendent is in no position to correct that state of affairs. The president's attitude must be viewed as a constraint under which the superintendent must attempt to run a department.

Likewise, it would be inappropriate for the president to blame a diminishing profit margin upon the fickleness and dishonesty of customers. This is a constraint under which the company must operate. The president should rather investigate the available courses of action that could diminish or overcome the effects of such traits.

The Problem-Finding Process Requires a Focus

The problem-finding process usually requires a focus that zeros in on the most important contributing factors before an attempt is made to identify minor causes. Those who have been faced with complex situations in which many factors were contributing to an outcome would readily subscribe to this guideline. The effective cashier will ignore the dime that rolls under the counter in order to stay close to the till. Similarly, the sales manager who feels that sales territories are improperly assigned may safely ignore this for the moment if he or she has also detected a self-defeating sales procedure that is antagonizing customers and losing sizable sales.

The Problem-Finding Process Deals with Probabilities Rather Than Absolutes

The problem-finding process will usually require that cause-effect relationships be approached from the standpoint of tendencies or probabilities, rather than absolutes. The tentativeness that characterizes effective problem finding has already been identified as one of the required attitudes for problem-finding and problem-solving processes. This tentativeness bears reemphasis. It is particularly appropriate in ill-structured and complex situations in which uncertainty and limited information are the norm. For example, few instances exist in which management is certain that a product-market decision is the best, that a complex production method is the one best way, that a motivation program will really meet the needs of the employees. Rather, the investigator should think in terms of: the *chances* are that, we *feel* our competitor will react, most people like Joe will *usually,* or we should have a 50 percent *probability.*

Some Observations Regarding the Depth of Problem-Finding Analysis

Operations analysis may be characterized as the "beginner's level" of problem finding. Here, decisions are identified that appear to have caused poor performance, and correction is made by substituting what appears to be a more suitable course of action. For example, when poor scheduling is identified, better schedules are substituted. When an ineffective policy is identified, a more appropriate policy is substituted. The cause is dealt with directly. But one additional step is missing.

The "senior level" of analysis asks the question, Why or how did the ineffectual decision get on the books? In other words, Why was that decision made in the first place? The rationale for an in-depth inquiry rests on the strong probability that the defects in the decision-making system that produced the poor decision are still in force. Unless these deeper causes are identified and corrected, they may produce more poor decisions. A probe into several levels of management may be necessary to unlock these deficiencies.

Regarding the Timing of Problem-Finding Activity

As is true in most areas of human endeavor, preventive steps are preferable to corrective actions after the damage has been done. Unfortunately, management problem-finding activity is usually reserved for after-the-fact situations; that is, management attempts a postmortem after profits, for example, have fallen, or after morale has dropped.

Forward-looking management, on the other hand, attempts to anticipate results and take preventive steps before harm has occurred. In these cases, results have not as yet occurred due to an inherent time lag between decisions and their effects. The purpose for an organizational audit, before the fact, is to determine whether the total system has any significant elements that may cause undesirable results in the future— for example, a conflict between policy and practice, inconsistency in strategy and some aspect of an implementation decision, an improper balance between short-run and long-run standards, or failure to deal with changes in the marketplace. These inconsistencies may have serious implications in the future if left undisturbed. Unfortunately, however, studies tend to indicate that executives prefer to focus on current problems rather than ill-defined future situations (Mintzberg), and that often there is not sufficient time for problem finding and solving in depth, particularly before-the-fact problem-finding processes.

References and Suggested Readings

REFERENCES

Ackoff, Russell L. "Management Misinformation System." *Management Science,* December, 1967, pp. B147–56.

Mayo, Elton. *The Social Problems of an Industrial Civilization.* London: Routledge, 1949. Pp. 60–76.

Mintzberg, Henry. "A New Look at the Chief Executive's Job." *Organizational Dynamics,* Winter, 1973.

Nichols, Ralph G. "Listening Is Good Business." *Management of Personnel Quarterly* 1, no. 2 (1962).

Perrow, Charles. *Organizational Analyses, A Sociological View.* Belmont, Calif.: Wadsworth Publishing Co., 1970. Ch. 3, 4, 5.

Van de Ven, Andrew, and Delbecq, Andre L. "Nominal versus Interacting Group Processes for Committee Decision-Making Effectiveness." *Academy of Management Journal,* June, 1971, pp. 203–12.

SUGGESTED READINGS

Art of Top Management: A McKinsey Anthology. New York: McGraw-Hill, 1970.

Juran, J. M. *Managerial Breakthrough: A Systematic Approach to Improving Management Performance.* New York: McGraw-Hill, 1965.

Kepner, Charles H., and Tregoe, Benjamin B. *The Rational Manager.* New York: McGraw-Hill, 1965.

Koontz, Harold. *Appraising Managers as Managers.* New York: McGraw-Hill, 1971.

Leavett, Harold J., Dell, William R., and Eyring, Henry B. *The Organizational World.* New York: Harcourt Brace Jovanovich, 1973.

Lorange, Peter, and Vancil, Richard F. "How to Design a Strategic Planning System." *Harvard Business Review,* Sept.-Oct., 1976, pp. 75–81.

Redden, W. J. *Effective Management by Objectives.* New York: McGraw-Hill, 1971.

2
Problem Finding, After the Fact

Introduction
    Why begin in operations?
    After-the-fact problem finding
    Problem finding in operations
The Phases of Problem Finding in Operations Analysis
    The relationship of the problem-finding phases with
        problem-finding approaches
    Some general problem-finding process observations and guides
        Complexity
        Detection
        Tentativeness
        Coverage
        Interpretation
        Independence
        Iteration
        Probability
        Order
Phase One—Results Analysis
    What are results?
        Outputs from operations—products and services
        Results that reflect the effects of product-service output
            upon the environment
        Results that reflect the by-products of activity
    The forms in which results may be reported
    The validity of results
    The future time factor of results
    The role of standards in results analysis

Appropriateness of standards
Target-setting considerations
    What kinds of events should be reflected in a forecast of the
        environmental factors?
    The random and nonrandom nature of environmental factors
    What factors should be included in a determination of
        resource capabilities?
Determining significant deviations
Phase Two—Activity-Interaction Analysis
    Things to look for
        Leadership styles
            Distinguishing leadership styles
            Distinguishing situations
            Task technology characteristics
            The leader's power
            Role expectations
            Synthesis
        Effort expended
        Communication patterns
        Work flow
        Business functions
        Behavioral patterns
        Adherence to policies and regulations
        Supervision
    Overview of activity-interaction phase
Phase Three—Resource Analysis
Phase Four—Reconstructing the Environmental Profile
Phase Five—Decision and Influence Analysis
    The formal decisions
    Critical variables for formulating strategic decisions
    Component parts of decisions—the strategic design decisions
        Objectives—Their component parts
            Needs
            Recipients
            States
            Priorities
            Creed
        External strategies—Their component parts
        Internal strategies—Their component parts
        Organization structure—Its component parts
            Factors to be considered in deciding upon an
                appropriate structure

Environmental states
Characteristics of the product and market
Characteristics of the technologies employed
Priorities
Some alternative arrangements for the division of work
Functional
Divisional
Venture
Some alternative arrangements for integration
Hierarchical authority
Competence
Grass roots
Some states that structure can effect
Some symptoms of inappropriate structural arrangements
Resource allocation—Its component parts
Component parts of decisions—control decisions
Work assignment—Its component parts
Conditions to be fostered—Formal job requirements
States sought—The human dimension
Authority delegation—Its component parts
Conditions to be fostered—Formal job requirements
States sought—The human dimension
Work standards—Their component parts
Work evaluations—Their component parts
Component parts of decisions—The tactical decisions
Determining linkages between decisions and results
Constructing a hierarchy of decisions
Selling the problem-finding analysis
Problem finding as a group effort
Some realities of human nature and the problem-finding
process
The silent-interacting group
Charting aids for operations analysis
Data sheet for results analysis, after the fact
Data sheet for activity-interaction analysis
Data sheet for after-the-fact resource capabilities analysis
Data sheet for an after-the-fact environment
profile
Decision and influence checklist
After-the-fact resumé sheet
Review of the model for problem finding, after the fact
Developing the hierarchy of causes (Decisions)

Introduction

X Corporation is on the brink of bankruptcy. Y Corporation is on strike. Z's sales are off 20 percent. Why? This chapter deals with a ferret skill for unravelling just such disturbing events in order to provide a meaningful, and operational, answer to the "why." By "operational" is meant the identification of causes that can be attacked so as to diminish or eliminate the adverse results. Specifically, a systematic as well as logical process is called for, together with some rules of the road to serve as guides for the problem-finding process. Such guides are as essential an adjunct to the process as those found for financial auditing or medical diagnosis.

Why Begin in Operations?

One of the most damaging tendencies of problem finders is to rely too heavily on personal opinions for identifying causes of poor performance. Judgments ought to be delayed until all the data that can be reclaimed are found. It is precisely for this reason that the problem-finding methodology is initiated at the results stage. This means that personalities and management decisions are among the very last concerns. Furthermore, the methodology is designed to discourage preconceived opinions of management styles or methods and to encourage situational thinking with respect to management techniques. When all the information about results, resources, activities, and environment has been collected, then an evaluation of management can be begun.

After-the-Fact Problem Finding

Chapter 2 is restricted to identifying causes for past unsatisfactory performance. This is after-the-fact analysis. The results have occurred. The causes are to be discovered in order to avoid a recurrence. Problem finding before the fact is, of course, a preferred approach to management; but human frailties, limited knowledge, and finite capabilities, unfortunately, make after-the-fact problem finding the more used perspective.

Problem Finding in Operations

One of the most useful concepts in research is the idea of the unit or the subject of research—i.e., the unit of analysis. This is an initial decision: Who or what is to be investigated? It may be a department, a division, or the company as a whole. Everything outside that particular unit is viewed as the environment.

The unit of analysis in the problem-finding, after-the-fact process is the operations area. Operations is "doing"-type work. It does not include the management of such work. Management makes decisions; doers physically carry out the decisions.

"Doing" work involves such activities as selling, carpentry, milling, buying, merchandising, record keeping, typing, public relations, engineering, hiring, training, paying, teaching, nursing, preaching, researching, and the like. Managing, in contrast, involves planning, organizing, controlling, decision making. These activities produce decisions on such matters as goals, standards, schedules, budgets, methods, strategies, policies, delegations, work assignments, and work sequences. They are intended to point the way or to structure or control "doing"-type work.

Managing and "doing" are also differentiated by the unique skills needed for each. To use selling skills in managing a group of salesmen is not the way to success. The star football player does not necessarily make a good football coach. The brilliant engineer does not necessarily have the qualifications for a career in managing engineers.

The Phases of Problem Finding in Operations Analysis

A four-step process for problem finding is based on the rather simple notion of an input output model. Complex situations are deliberately simplified in order to pinpoint the basic essentials of organized activity. The complications can be added later.

A given result can be viewed as a combination of environmental conditions, resource capabilities, and plans, plus the transformation process through which resources are changed into another, more valuable, form. In arriving at a result, there are four internal phases—plans, resources, activity, and output—and one external element, the environment. That is to say, there is a sequence of plans and resources, followed by activity, and finally the emerging output. For example, a new sales procedure (plan) is implemented by salesmen (resources). They engage in personal sales calls on prospective customers (activity), which lead to sales or perhaps to a no-sale (output) in the marketplace (the environment).

Problem finding reverses the sequence. It searches for information about adverse results (a no-sale situation), attempts to reconstruct the activity (sales call), looks closely at the capabilities of the resource (salesman), reconstructs the past environment, and attempts to identify those plans (e.g., sales procedures) that appear to have contributed to the significant deviation in results. Since many decisions in practice govern selling, the identification of the relevant cause becomes more involved than the example would suggest.

The phases of problem finding are as follows:

1. Analyze results—i.e., What happened? How did we do? The purpose: discover significant deviations from a standard. The notation that will be used for results is a square divided horizontally.

2. Activity-interaction analysis, i.e., the delayed playback. Its purpose: discover clues with respect to inappropriate activities or behaviors. The notation for activity that will be used is a rectangle.

3. Resource analysis—i.e., What were our capabilities?

The purpose: discover clues with respect to the existence of any resource inadequacies. The notation that will be used for resources is a square.

4. Environmental profile construction—i.e., What were the significant and relevant environmental conditions? Its purpose: discover the opportunities, constraints, and threats that actually existed. Did they differ from expectations? The notation that will be used for the environmental forces is a square open on the left.

5. Decision and influence analysis—i.e., What decisions or extraorganizational influences appear to be related to the clues that have been uncovered? What decisions should be reevaluated in view of environmental conditions, resource deficiencies, or inappropriate activities as they actually existed during the period under review? Its purpose: discover causes. The notation to be used for decisions and influences will be a diamond.

The five elements form a rather simplistic view of reality with all its manifold interrelationships; yet the model provides a convenient starting point for staging the problem-finding process.

The Relationship of the Problem-Finding Phases with Problem-Finding Approaches

In chapter 1 a number of approaches to problem finding were discussed. The symptoms approach focuses on the results cell. The leadership approach deals with the activity cell. In the example of a salesman using a new selling procedure, the leadership style of the boss would be discovered in the activity cell. The people, technology, information, materiel, and dollar approaches focus on the resource cell. The governance approach deals with the decision cell.

The problem-finding methodology views all approaches with a jaundiced eye, with the exception of the governance approach. The first seven, by and large, deal with symptoms and clues rather than with decisions. It is decisions that make things happen in the final analysis, and therefore, when things do go wrong, the chances are that decisions are the most significant contributing factor.

This approach does not "excuse" personal misconduct of the rank and file by saying that, basically, management causes poor performance. What this approach does imply, however, is that the manager is ultimately accountable for the performance of his subordinates; that there is only perhaps a 10 to 20 percent probability that environmental circumstances so overwhelmed management that it could not have reacted effectively. This is a hard-line position with respect to management, but it is felt to be a realistic and challenging one. In the final analysis, this position asks, Given the resources and the obstacles, how well has management utilized the potentials with which it had to work?

Some General Problem-Finding
Process Observations and Guides

COMPLEXITY

The problem finder deals with complexity. Unless the situation is well structured and can be numerically quantified with a high degree of certainty, the search will always be a difficult task. Often numerous other variables are involved, thus adding to the complexity. The search requires discrimination, namely, the identification of critical factors among the many that conceivably could have contributed to the state of affairs under investigation.

DETECTION

Rarely will a full set of data be thrust into the hands of the problem finder. Detection takes effort. The use of discerning questions at the right time to those closest to the action will often uncover surprising information. The exercise will test the problem finder's powers of perception, observation, and interpretation.

TENTATIVENESS

The problem finder will probably discover that the tendency to take premature positions becomes an obstacle to effectiveness. Information must be checked for accuracy and in some cases requires confirmation before acceptance. Apparently insignificant variables may become significant as one learns more of the case. Possible relationships and vital intervening factors may be ignored by the inflexibility that often is associated with premature judgment. Tentativeness is essential in order to encourage the skill of good listening until such time as sufficient data have been assembled.

COVERAGE

The omission of significant segments of organization activity in the information-collection process could result in inconclusive or misleading results. Specialization among problem finders could bring about a bias toward that area of expertise with an accompanying deemphasis of those fields in which the investigators feel less comfortable. Effectiveness in problem finding demands a reasonable coverage of all contributing activities.

INTERPRETATION

Data may be interesting, but their main utility arises only after they have been analytically examined and their relevance to the issues under investigation has been clarified. This involves the interpretation of facts, often the most provocative phase of problem finding.

INDEPENDENCE

The problem finder, under usual circumstances, will be subjected to pressures, and attempts will be made to influence his or her analysis. At times the chief enemy may be oneself; this occurs when one must sit in judgment over one's own stewardship as a manager. The temptation to cover up and protect one's own interest may become overwhelming. Objectivity can be fostered when problem finding is structured so as to facilitate relative freedom from undue influences of others and of self. There are no simple solutions for structuring such situations.

ITERATION

The problem-finding process is an iterative one. Clues uncovered in one area may lead to other interrelated areas. These, in turn, require analysis, and new information subsequently uncovered may point toward a reexamination of the original area.

PROBABILITY

Interrelationships among variables, cause-effect relationships between factors, coupled with uncertainty and incomplete information often require the problem finder to think in terms of probabilistic causes rather than deterministic or absolute causes. Statistical methods can often uncover an association between variables, but judgment must be used to infer a causal relationship.

ORDER

The entire problem-finding process demands an orderly, systematic approach. Some degree of structure facilitates an orderly search process in complex cases. It assists in maintaining a common focus particularly when several people are involved in the process.

Phase One—Results Analysis

Management by Results, a book written many years ago, asserts that, unless results of a person's efforts can be identified, the individual has probably not been contributing to the organization (Schleh). A more recent approach, *Management by Objectives* (MBO), focuses on goals, which become the standard against which results are judged (Odiorne). The dimension common to both approaches is results, and it is results that the problem-finding process analyzes initially.

What Are Results?

OUTPUTS FROM OPERATIONS—PRODUCTS AND SERVICES

Results, first of all, are the direct outputs of operations—namely, products or services. Operations, from the problem-finding viewpoint, is "doing"-type work. From this perspective, the marketing department produces results, as does production, personnel, or accounting—for example, $1 million in sales by marketing, a $50-per-unit cost of production, 10 percent employee turnover, or accounting cost data. All of the foregoing reflect results of operating systems in terms of product or service performed.

RESULTS THAT REFLECT THE EFFECTS OF
PRODUCT-SERVICE OUTPUT UPON THE ENVIRONMENT

Closely related to the actual product-service results of operations are the effects of the output upon the environment. These effects are an aspect of results that has grown in importance during recent years; they include the effect of corporate product-service upon its customers, the industry, its competitors, owners, or the community. For example, shoddy or potentially harmful products endanger the welfare of customers; success may be used to force out competition; high profits can give attractive returns to stockholders; and profits may provide a sound tax base for the community.

RESULTS THAT REFLECT THE
BY-PRODUCTS OF ACTIVITY

Results inevitably also arise as sought or unsought consequences of work—i.e., activity itself. These by-products affect the resources of the organization or the environment in some way. For example, work may be challenging or boring. When challenging, work may result in growth in employees' personal capabilities, which in turn may redound to the benefit of the company. If just plain hard work is required, it may produce character. If work is boring, it may result in high turnover. Handling and transporting the company's products result in equipment wear and tear. Idle capacity, i.e., no work, may cause plant deterioration.

Activity itself may affect the corporation's environment. The wood pulp manufacturing process can pollute rivers and waterways. Steel manufacturing can produce smoke pollution. Since such results cannot be directly deduced from product-service data alone, they must deliberately be sought out.

The Forms in Which Results May Be Reported

The form in which information is reported must be considered in order to make effective and accurate use of the data. Assume four departments that in sequence acquire materials, fabricate them, sell, and finally transport the product to the customer. The results of these operations may be reported as value added by each department, or they may be stated as cumulative values reflecting the contributions of all four departments. Value-added results are particularly useful when the performance of a single department is under review; cumulative reports are needed when the entire organization is under review.

The income statement focuses on costs and benefits, where expenses represent costs and income forms the benefits. However, the income statement provides few clues as to the "bene-fit" contribution of most departments, since their results appear only as "costs." One must therefore ascertain the output benefits—for example, the number of units produced.

A comparative balance sheet allows the problem finder to compute changes in such resource values as cash, plant, equipment, inventory, materials, or supplies. Important resources, however, are customarily omitted: company dealers, company and product image, locations, and the skills and capacities of employees.

Results may also be provided as "raw" or as "comparative" results. An absolute cost or income figure is a "raw" result. It stands alone. It provides few clues as to the effectiveness or efficiency of the company unless comparative data are also provided. Whenever comparisons are provided, however, the problem finder should be on the alert. Here is where manipulators figure, despite the fact that figures may be accurate. It is relatively easy to substantiate a position by using the "appropriate" denominator in a ratio. Last year, for example, Company A may have sold 100 units. This year it sold 125. The sales manager is complimented for the 25 percent increase. If, however, he had reported that during this same period industry sales had increased 50 percent, he might have been looking for a different position.

Foreman Jones receives a promotion for reducing his costs by 10 percent over a two-year period. The following year Foreman Smith, his successor, records a 5-percent increase in costs. Who has done the better job? If the department simply compares costs with those of the previous year, Foreman Jones wins. Further analysis, however, may disclose that labor rates had increased or that the present foreman was forced to spend extra sums to put the equipment back on a regular preventive maintenance schedule.

The measure of profitability is another interesting illustration of the critical nature of the denominator as well as the numerator in ratio analysis (Dearden, Henrici, or Henderson and Dearden). Return on investment (ROI) is the ratio of profit (assume a net-profit-after-tax figure) to net investment (after deducting accumulated depreciation from total investment). This ratio is a valuable guide for evaluating performance as long as those who use it understand its peculiar subtleties.

The numerator, first of all, is the amount of profit. It represents operating efficiency—the transformation of resources into outputs—and organization effectiveness with respect to the customer or the environment; that is, it is the difference between income and costs. In order to compare company ROI to plan, to a historical figure, or to that of a competitor, a consistent treatment of expenses and income must be maintained for both the current figure and for the one to which it is compared. Inconsistencies can arise in the treatment of certain costs. Costs may be arbitrarily postponed, capitalized, or written off during the year incurred. The arbitrary postponement of normal expenditures can achieve a lower cost profile than would otherwise be possible. Extraordinary costs or incomes that are not directly attributable to one fiscal period, or a corporate financial structure that incurs interest adjustments to income, can provide distortions when comparisons are attempted.

Denominator inconsistencies are also prevalent. Here the investment base represents the assets available or devoted to the production of profit. Common distortions occur when different depreciation methods are utilized or when inflation distorts historical cost figures.

The investment base produces another problem in evaluating managers. Major investment decisions may not have been made by managers who are to implement them. Either the decisions were made at a higher level or the decision maker no longer occupies a position of direct accountability. Since these decisions are long-run, reaping potential benefits and cost write-offs over many years, it is quite conceivable that no one is currently responsible for some of the investment-base decisions. This is particularly true for capital-intensive industries such as the railroads or the steel industry, whose ROI figures have become meaningless for comparative purposes. Schiff and Schiff recommend, for example, that accounts receivable and inventory should under some circumstances be used instead of total assets as a base for evaluating managers (Schiff and Schiff). The managers would then be held accountable for the utilization of resources over which they had direct control.

Holden, Pederson, and Germane report that some companies use the *gross* investment figure *before* depreciation inasmuch as these companies feel that facilities are usually maintained at a high productive level during their useful life cycle. The reserve for depreciation is designed primarily to provide for obsolescence rather than reflect depreciation. On the other hand, when net depreciated value is used, the investment base varies for each period despite the fact that the *productive* value of the asset is kept constant (Holden, et al.).

The Validity of Results

The accuracy of results represents a second test that the problem finder must face. Most results, fortunately, are not pure myth, but, nevertheless, they can represent only partial accounts, half-truths, or secondary, hearsay accounts. First-hand or primary data are preferable to secondary data; full disclosure is preferable to half-truths; and facts are better than opinions.

Results must also be checked against their time of occurrence. It would appear manifestly misleading to base an evaluation on an employee's performance several years ago. Yet the halo effect or its opposite unfortunately continues to play an important role in some performance evaluations.

The Future Time Factor of Results

A final dimension of results is the future time factor. Perhaps of all the conceivable pitfalls in results analysis, this is the one that inhibits the continuance of truly outstanding performance by many managers.

Most results contain elements of short-run and long-run activities. Some activities do not reap manifest rewards until years later. Other activities provide immediate achievements. Managers often fail to maintain a reasonable balance between short-run and long-run considerations, partially due to restraints imposed upon them, but also because of the press of short-run personal needs and goals. Superiors may also contribute to this dilemma by giving lip service to long-run product research and management development activities, for example, but then defining annual goals in a way that forces a short-run perspective, excluding any real efforts in long-run activities. For the problem finder, the implications of such situations are that he or she must attempt to differentiate results in terms of immediate, visible achievements vis-à-vis those that do not provide immediate visibility. In effect, the latter become work-in-process and must be considered in any equitable evaluation process.

The Role of Standards in Results Analysis

It is practically impossible to evaluate performance unless a criterion is available against which to compare results. Raw results, such as $1 million in sales last year, provide little indication as to whether this achievement represents meritorious or deficient performance. Due in part to the neglect of explicitly stated goals, management by objectives (MBO) rapidly became a popular approach for management. On the other hand, the mere presence of goals does not ensure that standards are appropriate.

The problem, therefore, seems to be one of providing a reasonable standard against which to measure performance, and setting this standard before activity is commenced. In most instances, positive motivational forces are unleashed when employees have targets toward which to shoot, know what is expected of them, and can see potential rewards based upon the achievement of these goals. Participation in the goal-setting process may provide some additional motivational thrust (Odiorne).

Appropriateness of Standards

The importance of control mechanisms, of which standards are an integral part, does not always appear to be as evident to managers as it probably should be. In the experience of some management consultants, more problems arise out of malfunctions in the control function of management than from any other single management activity.

An evaluation of performance must be based upon appropriate criteria. If the standards are inappropriate, evaluations become meaningless and misleading and can severely upset the morale of the employees. One important mission of the problem finder is to ensure that the standards are proper. This section of "Results Analysis" will briefly review the kinds of considerations that can influence the setting of standards.

To begin with, standards have their origin in the fond hopes, ambitions, dreams, or "states" that management leaders would like to achieve for their organization as well as, perhaps, for themselves. Such states could include profitability, effectiveness, growth, acceptance, safety, flexibility, adaptability, strength, independence, productivity, liquidity, solvency, efficiency, responsiveness, satisfaction, or happiness. Few fail to seek such attributes. They are often defined as goals or objectives. Very little is really accomplished, however, by their simple identification. Few organizations seek their opposite: inflexibility, inefficiency, unprofitableness, instability, and so on. One problem that arises with these ambitions is that many of these states are interdependent. Becoming too efficient in certain customer-sensitive product-service areas could decrease market effectiveness; extreme responsiveness to customer wants could, on the other hand, diminish efficiency and profitableness; growth may bring all kinds of problems in reduced flexibility, responsiveness, or human satisfaction. The achievement of each state involves attendant costs and benefits, which often affect other desired states. A balance is to be achieved in order to avoid negative results that outweigh the benefits to be derived from some course of action.

Many decisions are necessary to arrive at "state" achievement. Decisions make the attainment of states operational. Decisions are the manager's instruments for state attainment. When organizations divide themselves into many subunits in order to take advantage of specialization, suboptimizations tend to arise; that is, functional departmental goals do not mesh with the ultimate states the organization is attempting to achieve. The departmental perspective seems to rule. To discourage that kind of suboptimization, countertargets are needed. For example, a sales quota could be kept under a profit constraint; a standard production cost, coupled with quality standards.

For the problem finder, decisions should aim toward a "state" that is to be achieved, and such states need visibility —that is, to be known. Ideally, the purpose of every decision should be formally recorded, but this is rarely done. Such a practice would facilitate a reexamination of the continued effectiveness of a decision. When a situation changes, a decision may no longer be the most effective one. For example, a no-smoking rule is unnecessary when the materials currently in use are not flammable.

After the state to be achieved is known, the measuring instrument becomes the next consideration. The problem that arises here is that the yardstick in use may not measure the state that is to be achieved. For example, the acquisition of a new fleet of trucks may have as its objective an increase in the safety of operation. But the yardstick that may be utilized, for example, is cost per mile of operation, and obviously that does not directly measure the purpose for which the fleet was secured.

A final consideration in standard setting concerns the points on the yardstick that are used to evaluate performance. Preferably, a range of points should be specified that is reasonable and that distinguishes between adequate and meritorious performance. For example, a 10 to 13 percent return on investment could be chosen to represent a ROI target range. Sliding target ranges form another device that can be utilized to provide goals based on various possible market conditions.

When the problem finder discovers that standards are absent, an important finding has actually been made. Yet even when standards are explicitly provided, they may still be inappropriate. Inappropriateness or incompleteness can occur with respect to the target, the yardstick, or a decision that does not make explicit its purpose. The last kind of problem can be identified by asking such discerning questions as, "Why are you doing this?" "Why are you doing it in this way?" If the answer comes back, "I don't know," "It's policy," or "We've always done it this way," then a deeper probe is probably necessary.

In results analysis the problem finder has the first opportunity to uncover clues or tentative causes, although the primary purpose of such analysis is to identify significant deviations from standards. These clues or potential causes include such problems as insufficient results data across the broad spectrum of organization activity, undiscoverable aims, inappropriate measurement instruments, or unrealistic targets.

The next section will briefly review target-setting considerations in order that the problem finder may be aware of some of the important determiners of targets.

Target-Setting Considerations

The target is determined from two sets of relatively unrelated data. The first set is composed of information about resource capabilities required to achieve some stated goal; the second set, information about the environment. Both sets of information relate to a defined future planning period.

Planning premises, under which work is to be conducted, are derived from these data.

A new-car dealer, for example, in setting a sales quota would probably consider the capabilities of the sales personnel, and the company's financial capacities, lot location, and image on the one hand and, on the other hand, the new-car market, the local economic situation, and competitors' activities. In effect the dealer has related corporate resource capabilities with environmental opportunities and constraints in deciding upon certain performance expectations for a future planning period. This process is illustrated in Fig. 2.1.

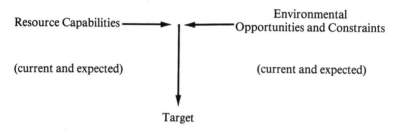

FIG. 2.1. THE TARGET-SETTING PROCESS

WHAT KINDS OF EVENTS SHOULD BE REFLECTED IN A FORECAST OF THE ENVIRONMENTAL FACTORS?

In order to identify relevant environmental factors, it is helpful to recognize that changes in the environment, which the forecaster hopes to predict, arise from rare, abnormal, or unpredictable events and from normal but also unpredictable occurrences. Unpredictability here means that some uncertainty is present. Now, there appears to be a reasonable consensus that a forecast should reflect the "normal" events, but not the "abnormal" occurrences (Schleh). The rationale for this position is that targets are intended to hold the executive responsible for dealing with normal business risks, but not such abnormal events as would be included under the label of acts of God or acts of the public enemy. Normal events refer

to such factors as competitors' activities, consumer preferences, or those reflected by the economic indicators. Some of
the latter have lead or lag characteristics that actually aid in
arriving at a forecast. This dichotomy is illustrated in Fig. 2.2.

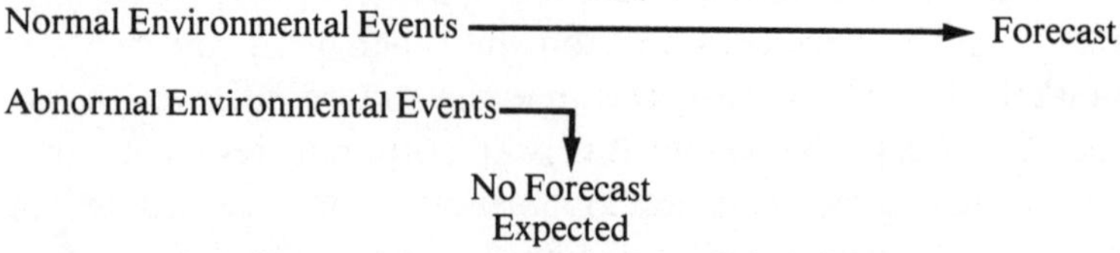

Normal Environmental Events ——————————————→ Forecast

Abnormal Environmental Events——┐
                               ↓
                        No Forecast
                        Expected

FIG. 2.2.   ENVIRONMENTAL EVENTS AND
            FORECASTING

Normal events can be further refined into those over which
the manager can exercise some influence and those that are
beyond his control. At times a decision as to whether some
variable is discretionary or nondiscretionary depends upon
the desires, capabilities, values, or inventiveness of the manager. A decision to advertise, in effect, is saying that consumer preferences are a discretionary factor that the manager
is willing and able to influence. Competitor pricing practices
may be neutralized by some companies, while other organizations may simply accept competitive actions as beyond their
range of influence. The point is that, once the normal events
are forecast, a decision must be made as to whether or not
the organization is willing or able to influence the selected
variables. If a decision to influence is made, the original forecast must be amended to reflect any expected changes emanating from the decision (see Fig. 2.3).

THE RANDOM AND NONRANDOM NATURE
OF ENVIRONMENTAL FACTORS

Some environmental factors can also be viewed from the
perspective of whether their variations exhibit randomness or
reflect systematic, regularized change, i.e., nonrandomness.
    The nonrandom environmental variables are those that the

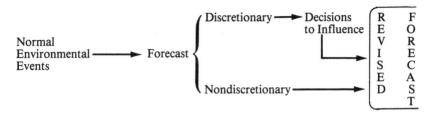

FIG. 2.3. DISCRETIONARY AND NONDISCRETIONARY
VARIABLES IN FORECASTING

management practitioner, the economist, the sociologist, and the psychologist have in the past associated with variations in performance. The point is that these environmental forces possess characteristics that enable those affected by them to (1) recognize their regularized pattern of change and (2) take some action for exploiting, neutralizing, or adapting to their changing values, with varying degrees of success. For example, some consumer buying behavior varies systematically with the seasons of the year or with changes in disposable personal income. In some industries, competitors react to the actions of a recognized leader in a fairly consistent pattern.

The random variables in the environment are those whose patterns of behavior have not been discovered or have not been isolated as distinguishable forces. They may also include the very short-run variations of essentially nonrandom forces. Such short-run variations reflect, in part, the inherent instability of environmental forces in terms of hourly, daily, or even weekly variations. Over longer periods, patterns often develop, and the variations can then be considered nonrandom. Often the short-run variations are so numerous, or individually have so little effect, that it would be economically unwise to attempt to influence them. The rationale for this position is that these minor variations tend to average out over a somewhat longer period of time.

Not all short-run variations should be treated as outside the realm of consideration. For example, experience with special incentives offered by some retailers to induce customers to

change their buying schedules, particularly the timing of purchases, indicates that an apparent randomness is, in fact,
subject to some influence. However, in the absence of such
capabilities, random variables tend to distort results when
viewed in the very short run. For example, assume that a sales
quota of fifty units per month is sought and the month has
twenty-five work days. Daily evaluation of results based on an
average of two sales per day simply does not take into consideration the reality of random variables operating in the
environment. Result variations from the average could also
be associated with random variations in the efforts and capabilities of the human resource, the subject of the next topic.
Our forecasting model so far is illustrated in Fig. 2.4.

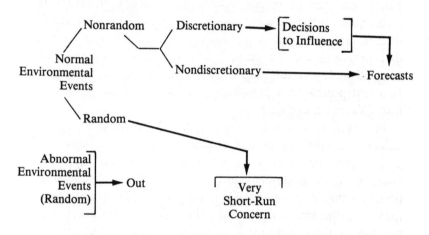

FIG. 2.4.   RANDOM AND NONRANDOM VARIABLES
            IN FORECASTING

WHAT FACTORS SHOULD BE INCLUDED IN A
DETERMINATION OF RESOURCE CAPABILITIES?

The employee, as one of a number of resources committed
to a venture, has acquired certain capabilities. Assuming
employees have been selected for positions appropriate to their

abilities, past performance may provide a rough approximation of their capabilities, other things being equal. However, it is also true that several individuals with similar abilities may perform quite differently. These differences can be attributed in part to the nonrandom factors that aid or abet their performance. These could involve needs, values, beliefs, desires, personal goals, attitudes, or sentiments. They have nothing directly to do with innate or learned abilities. Most of us have observed a highly rated team lose to a fired-up, class B team. Attitudes here probably played a major role.

Managers may view such nonrandom factors as either discretionary or nondiscretionary. Management texts and training programs are replete with methods for tapping the potential energies of employees through various motivational techniques. What is suggested by them is, first, that needs, desires, and personal goals can be determined and, second that programs can be devised that will cause employees to respond with increased effort. The cover of a recent motivation text portrayed a carrot to illustrate this idea of motivation (Vroom and Deci).

In practice, however, while some companies do regard values and attitudes as discretionary variables to be tapped or changed, others have experienced little success with such attempts or have simply considered these factors nondiscretionary—that is, beyond their control. In addition, companies may be reluctant to deal with values and attitudes not only because of their inability to affect such deep-seated feelings but also on moral grounds.

Employee performance also exhibits the effects of random factors. These phenomena are easy to observe. No one works at the same speed with a constant quality throughout the eight hours in a day. Management has not actually considered all such factors random. The institution of the coffee break, for example, was supposedly intended, in part, to stimulate more consistent performance. The point is that performance in one hour, one day, or perhaps even one week reflects the effects of these random variables, which are products of the inherent nature of people. Fig. 2.5 diagrams random and nonrandom influences on employee performance and their effect on capabilities.

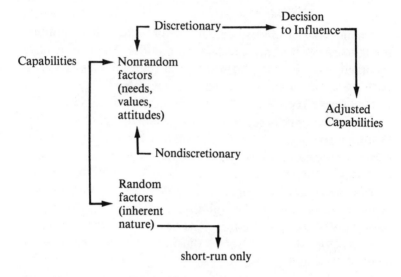

FIGURE 2.5.   Random and Nonrandom Influences on Capabilities

The target range for departmental performance is finally determined by coupling the capabilities of all committed resources as adjusted by management decisions with the forecasts of opportunities, constraints, and obstacles in the environment.

The purpose of providing this rather rapid review of target-setting considerations has been to pinpoint, perhaps in a highly abstract fashion, the crucial determiners of appropriate targets. The process of target setting, however, cannot be mechanized or highly structured. Capabilities cannot be easily quantified. Relating capabilities to economic forecasts of environmental opportunities or obstacles is a highly judgmental process. However, this brief discussion is intended to alert the problem finder to some of the more important considerations in determining the appropriateness of targets, in case a probe in that direction appears necessary or desirable.

Determining Significant Deviations

Results analysis has now come to its final step—determining whether or not significant deviations from standards have occurred. The accuracy of the decision will be based in large part upon the quality of the problem finder's preliminary evaluation of results and standards.

Results can now be compared to standards. When an appropriate target range has been provided, results that fall outside the range are significant deviations, unless the difference is so small that, in effect, it can be attributed to random factors. Then no further action is called for. When a significant deviation has occurred, however, an assignable cause or causes must be operating.

As a final note, it must again be emphasized that results analysis considers a broad spectrum of results to ensure that departmental suboptimizations are not occurring or that the organization is not maintaining an inappropriate balance among its responsibilities to customers, owners, and community. In considering a broad spectrum of results, one should for example look for compensating events that hide unsatisfactory performance. For example, targeted costs may have been achieved when an unexpected savings in labor costs compensated for increased material costs due to sloppy processing. Unless both labor and material costs are analyzed, the latter deficiency would go unnoticed until such time as labor costs behave in a more normal fashion.

When targets are proper and results fall outside the target range, a significant deviation has probably occurred. This is the stimulus for problem-finding activity to move to its next phase: an attempt to uncover any activity-interaction clues that appear related to the significant deviation.

Phase Two—Activity-Interaction Analysis

The focus in the second phase of problem finding, after the fact, is on the activity-interaction cell that precedes in time the significant deviations. Despite the fact that an accurate playback is usually impossible, recollections, as well as subsequent observations of similar activities, will probably provide some information clues. The chances are that nothing much of substance has changed in the meantime.

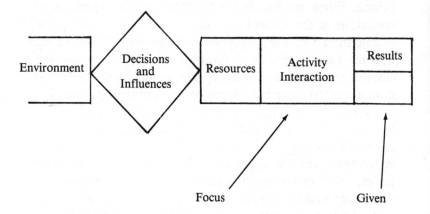

FIG. 2.6. THE FOCUS OF PHASE TWO IN THE
PROBLEM FINDING MODEL

The activity-interaction cell reflects the consequences of the strengths and weaknesses of the resources assigned to an activity, the efficacy of management decisions, or the effects of other influences that may have been directed toward the activity cell. Its place in the business process is shown in Fig. 2.6.

The activity cell is an exceedingly complex phenomenon. In essence it is composed of a long interconnected series of causes and effects as illustrated in Fig. 2.7.

The work-flow chart illustrates a series of activities with

intermediate results which together may constitute the subject of an activity-interaction analysis. The purpose for activity-interaction analysis is to uncover inappropriate activities, interactions, or behaviors that relate to the significant deviation. The chart also illustrates some resource and decision inputs and the final sales result for the month under review. An obvious deficiency in the illustrated activity-interaction sequence is that the credit department took unilateral action without advising sales that a credit problem existed. When the search for inappropriate behaviors is successful, as in the above case, then an attempt must be made to determine why the inappropriate behavior arose. This may lead the problem finder to some other behavioral or activity clues or to some resource deficiencies, but ultimately the path should lead to some inappropriate management decisions.

Things to Look For

Several categories of possible inappropriate activities and interactions can be suggested as a guide for the problem finder. Each of these will be briefly elaborated upon:

1. Leadership style
2. Degree of effort expended by employees (motivation)
3. Communication patterns
4. Work flow
5. Business functions
6. Behavioral patterns
7. Adherence to policies and regulations
8. Supervision

LEADERSHIP STYLES

The reason for observing leadership style in a problem situation is to make some preliminary assessment of its appropriateness. An important premise in problem finding is that appropriateness of leadership style depends upon the kind of situation in which it is used. This entails identifying the

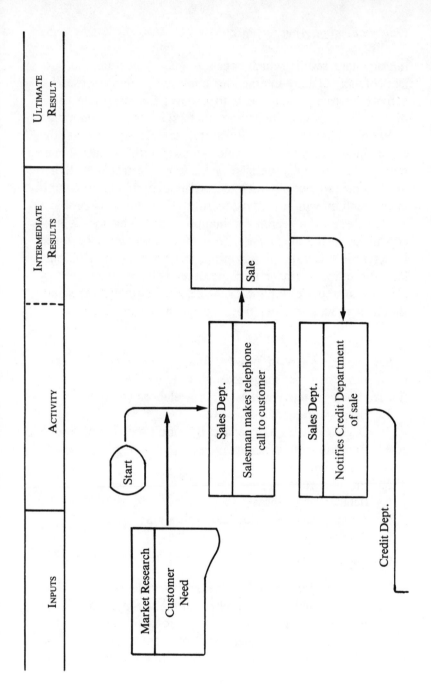

| INPUTS | ACTIVITY | INTERMEDIATE RESULTS | ULTIMATE RESULT |

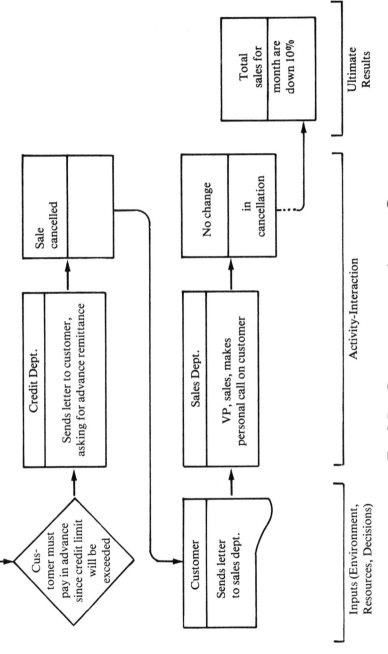

FIG. 2.7. COMPONENTS OF AN ACTIVITY CELL

style, distinguishing situations, and understanding the relationship between style used in a particular situation and organization effectiveness.

Distinguishing Leadership Styles. Although leadership style can be observed, no real consensus exists as to categories of leadership style. It appears, however, that a distinguishing feature for the problem finder would be the *primary* expertise exhibited in a leader's behavorial patterns. In most cases, a manager's primary skill is in one of three areas: (1) the skill demonstrated in responding to the technical aspects of the task, including administrative skills for setting schedules, work flows, procedures, or methods; (2) the skill shown in responding to employees on a one-to-one basis; (3) the skill shown in responding to employees on a group basis.

It is quite conceivable that a particular skill may have been developed as a result of a manager's specific concern for getting the job done (achieving some tangible product or service results), or a concern for meeting the needs of people individually or in a group setting. Irrespective of how or why certain skills may have been acquired, the important point is that wide differences in leadership style do exist and that organization effectiveness depends, in part, upon whether or not the leadership style exercised is appropriate for the situation in which it is used. Fortunately, there is a growing body of empirical knowledge that provides some insight into the style that tends to be most effective in a given situation.

Table 2.1 identifies some of the important behaviors characteristic of each style. Related to the three categories of behavior are the various requirements of different types of tasks. Some jobs require close attention to technical detail in order to achieve organization goals. Other tasks require close attention to people's needs—i.e., the provision of an open and supportive climate accompanied by varying degrees of job freedom—in order to meet objectives. Yet other situations require close attention to the provision of an organizational

Table 2.1. Leadership Styles and Their Related Behaviors

Task-Oriented Behaviors	Person-to-Person Behaviors	Group-Oriented Behaviors
Commands	Discusses	Holds Group Meetings
Decides unilaterally	Consults and then decides	Looks for a consensus, but may make the decision
Usually initiates events	Either party initiates an event	Any group member may initiate an event
Is impersonal in his relationships	Practices personal relationships	Practices team relationships
Maintains his independence	Is dependent on the individual	Is dependent on the group
Identifies with the task	Identifies with the individual	Identifies with the group
Uses close supervision	Uses general supervision	Coaches
Punishes nonconformity	May ignore nonconformity or may expect an individual to grow psychologically and technologically from the experience	Expects the group to learn from the situation
Uses his authority and power	Uses his authority and power with considerable discretion	Keeps a low authority-power profile
Practices downward communications	Practices two-way communications	Practices open, circular, or crosswise communication patterns
Looks for conformity	Looks for personal commitment to work	Looks for team involvement in the work

climate that fosters teamwork in order that the organization task can be best accomplished (Fiedler; Reddin).

Distinguishing Situations. Although there is also a lack of consensus as to the factors that distinguish situations adequately for problem finding, it appears that, for the most common organization situation, these factors include: (1) the technology underlying a task, (2) the power vested in the manager, and (3) the kind of leadership style expected by those involved (Fiedler; Reddin).

Task Technology Characteristics. Table 2.2 identifies several attributes of task technology. Three of these refer directly to the technology; one, to the end result itself; and the last three to the manager's overall task responsibilities in supervising the exercise of related or unrelated technologies. Task technologies are distinguished along the dimension of *difficulty* (knowledge requirements); *confidence* in or *reliability* of the technology (the degree of uncertainty with respect to the effectiveness of the technology); and *change* (the susceptibility of the technology to obsolescence). The manager's responsibilities with respect to the supervision of technologies are distinguished in terms of *interdependencies* (the degree to which jobs under the manager's command are dependent upon each other); *scope* (the breadth and depth of the manager's responsibilities—e.g., size, many vs. few technological areas, many vs. few products, etc.); *dependency* (the degree of the manager's dependency upon subordinates for information prerequisite to decision-making). The single attribute, *goal clarity,* refers to the precision with which the end result can, in fact, be measured.

Generally, the task-oriented style is required for organization effectiveness when task conditions approximate those listed on the left side of the continuum in Table 2.2; the person-to-person style, for intermediate positions; and the group style for task circumstances approximating those shown on the right side of the continuum. These assignments are not

TABLE 2.2. TASK TECHNOLOGY CHARACTERISTICS

TASK ATTRIBUTES	RANGE OF VALUES		
Difficulty level of the technology	Simple (routine) ◄———————►		Complex (professional or scientific)
Confidence level in the technology (reliability and validity)	Certain (best way) ◄———————►		Uncertain (little confidence)
Susceptibility of technology to *CHANGE*	Limited (slow) ◄———————►		Unlimited (rapid)
Goal Clarity of task	Clear (measurable) ◄———————►		Obscure (not readily measurable)
Interdependency of jobs in manager's area of responsibility	High (Each job serially dependent upon the preceding one; e.g., the assembly line) ◄———	(Jobs largely independent)	———► Low (each job interacts with every other job throughout the task cycle)
Scope of manager's overall task responsibilities	Narrow (small size, few areas) ◄———————►		Wide (large size, many areas)
Dependency of leader upon his subordinates	Limited (leader knows best, understands technology, has access to all necessary information) ◄———	(leader capable of making decisions, but dependent on subordinates for necessary information)	———► Unlimited (group evaluation of information will bring out implications not possible under a unilateral evaluation)

absolute, but reasonable first approximations. Extenuating circumstances can change the assignments.

More specifically, the task-oriented style is appropriate when personal discretion of employees must be avoided, when task freedoms would undermine the technology, when standardization is needed, and when the leader is the most knowledgeable person on the floor.

The person-to-person orientation is generally more effective when personal discretion on the part of skilled and professional employees is necessary, when creativity is a necessary adjunct, when the manager does not possess the full technical expertise, when critical information is generated by the subordinates, and when this knowledge is a prerequisite for effective decision making.

The group orientation is generally appropriate when collective evaluation by all members of a group would produce a better decision than evaluation solely by the manager. Here the task is complex, the manager does not have the technical expertise of his subordinates, the information generated requires a collective evaluation, and the decision, under some circumstances, may prove to be superior when arrived at by consensus of the group.

The Leader's Power. The second situational factor gives recognition to the power possessed by the leader—i.e., the ability to make things happen by granting awards, imposing penalties, or influencing supervisors.[1] Under the task-oriented style, position power is usually a necessary adjunct for effectiveness, while under the other styles the negative persuaders associated with power are not relied upon to the same extent. It appears that power is not as critical to those leadership styles as to the task-oriented style. Nevertheless, it should be recognized that leading from a strong power base, albeit sel-

---

1. F. E. Fiedler, in *A Theory of Leadership Effectiveness,* considers position power the least important among his three situational factors: leader-member relations, task structure, and position power.

dom invoked, is quite different from a situation in which this capability is lacking.

Technology, once determined, is usually costly and difficult to change drastically. In contrast, some business organizations find position power more susceptible to change. There are important exceptions, particularly, at the foreman level where the need for uniformity or the implications of independent action are so severe that power restrictions are common.

Role Expectations. The kind of style expected by those involved (subordinates, superiors, peers, or the particular culture) can also play an important role in organization effectiveness.[2] It is almost axiomatic that, when expectations run counter to the leader's style, problems will arise, but managing such expectations is a difficult and complicated process.

A Synthesis. The most effective leadership style varies with situational factors. The problem of matching the style with the situation may be within the discretionary control of many organizations, at least in the long run. The technology situational factor may well be the most important variable for determining the most appropriate style, when organization effectiveness is the prime issue. A divergence between the manager's style and the style suggested by the technology may become a serious matter. A conflict between style and expectations may be easier to identify than solve. Expectations usually are not under control of management, although company actions may be an important determiner of such expectations. With the final addition of the power variable, measured simply as strong or weak, eighteen possible situational profiles emerge.

Table 2.3 diagrams the various profiles. Eight are rather rare and can be disregarded. They would not normally develop under the specified technological circumstances. Three

2. Adapted from W. J. Reddin, *Managerial Effectiveness.*

TABLE 2.3. VARIOUS COMBINATIONS OF SITUATIONAL VARIABLES AND RESULTING LEADERSHIP STYLES, CLASSIFIED BY EFFECTIVENESS

Leadership Styles

Situation Variables / Profile / Classification	Task — Task (Strong)	Task — Task (Weak)	Task — One to One (Strong)	Task — One to One (Weak)	Task — Group (Strong)	Task — Group (Weak)	One to One — Task (Strong)	One to One — Task (Weak)	One to One — One to One (Strong)	One to One — One to One (Weak)	One to One — Group (Strong)	One to One — Group (Weak)	Group — Task (Strong)	Group — Task (Weak)	Group — One to One (Strong)	Group — One to One (Weak)	Group — Group (Strong)	Group — Group (Weak)
Situational Profile — Technol.	T	T	T	T	T	T	O	O	O	O	O	O	G	G	G	G	G	G
Expecta.	T	T	O	O	G	G	T	T	O	O	G	G	T	T	O	O	G	G
Power	S	W	S	W	S	W	S	W	S	W	S	W	S	W	S	W	S	W
Ideal	*								*								*	
Variance probably insignificant										*								*
Rare					*	*	*	*			*	*	*	*				
Situations leading to poor performance		1 *	2 *	3 *											4 *	5 *		

Key   T: Task
  O: One-to-One
  G: Group
  S: Strong
  W: Weak

profiles represent the ideal leadership for the task technology involved. Two situations that feature weak power positions are less than ideal but do not reflect critical variances. Finally, five profiles remain in which the leadership situation may lead to poor performance. The best way to deal with such situations is not always evident. In the first of these (1) the weak power position is associated with a task technology and task expectations. In situations (2) and (3) the technology calls for a task-oriented style while the employees expect or want a one-to-one style—a common phenomenon. The difference between (2) and (3) is that of a strong and a weak power position. The latter case can become most distressing, while the former can probably be resolved with a task-oriented style, other things being equal. Situations (4) and (5) are less common; the technology calls for a group-oriented style, employees are seeking a one-to-one style, and the power positions are strong and weak, respectfully.

All the listed dichotomies are somewhat artificial; situations within each classification actually vary by degrees. To remedy unsatisfactory performance, all such "gray areas" should be reviewed in a search for the most practicable methods of improving the situation.

EFFORT EXPENDED

A great deal can be learned about the state of motivation of employees by observing their day-to-day activities and interactions. Probably one of the most meaningful clues to the degree of motivation is the amount of effort exerted in organization-related activities. As a general rule, employees will expend more effort if (1) they think their increased efforts can affect their performance, (2) they think that improved performance leads to rewards, and (3) they value the expected reward. As a prerequisite to the above, certain conditions must be met: (4) employees have the required capabilities for the job expected, (5) employees value using these abilities, (6) employees correctly understand what results are to be achieved by their efforts, and (7) feedback is available to employees regarding their performance accomplishments.[3]

When questionable activities are observed—for example, when employees engage in excessive horseplay, meticulously follow rules and procedures, waiting for precise instructions each time before proceeding with work, or show a spirit of disinterest or argumentation—such clues may well point to motivational problems stemming from one of the seven causal areas enumerated above.

Examples of the causal areas are as follows: (1) An employee would find little relationship between making more sales calls and actually selling more when the competitive product is superior and lower priced. (2) An employee would see little relationship between selling more and receiving a promotion when seniority is the basic criterion for promotion. (3) An employee would experience a little motivational thrust if promotion is the expected reward, but he or she has little interest in becoming a desk-bound sales manager. (4) Increased motivation will not result when a supervisor lacks the capabilities for his or her job. (5) Performance will probably suffer when an engineer is expected to cultivate prospective customers but would prefer to use his or her abilities in creating new designs. (6) An employee who misunderstands what is expected is unlikely to perform well. (7) Motivation will usually be hindered when employees have no concrete evidence of the caliber of their performance.

COMMUNICATION PATTERNS

The sociometric patterns in communications are considered by some to play a significant role in organization effectiveness (Whyte). The issues are these: Which party normally tends

---

3. These variables are largely suggested in "Job design and employee motivation" by Edward E. Lawler, III and "Antecedent attitudes of effective managerial performance" by Edward W. Lawler, III and Lyman Porter, both in *Management and Motivation,* edited by Victor H. Vroom and Edward L. Deci.

to initiate activity or initiate interaction with respect to others, how frequently does this occur, and what is the degree of dominance portrayed in taking or keeping control of the interaction? While such phenomena could be considered part of leadership style, they relate equally well to subordinate behavior. They also can serve to differentiate jobs. Because the interaction pattern is very significant and readily observable, this aspect of communication warrants separate attention.

One of the most important differences among jobs is the degree of interaction required. For example, William F. Whyte discovered that job success for a waitress coincides closely with her ability to initiate the activity-interaction pattern with respect to her customers. Inability to develop the interaction pattern required by the job often leads to decreased performance. Likewise, a high rate of activity initiations by a superior upon a subordinate, by a solicitor upon a customer, or by a professional upon a patient when the situational requirements do not call for such interactions may also adversely affect performance. For example, some psychologists and medical practitioners seem to have a persistent tendency to direct, initiate, and control activity-interaction with respect to their patients. This may lead to a less reliable diagnosis. On the other hand, many selling jobs demand this very trait for job success.

The activity-interaction pattern displayed by an individual may well be a manifestation of personality traits, and to that extent the interaction pattern tends to be an enduring characteristic. It then becomes an integral part of the person's work style or leadership style.

Several areas of concern may therefore become apparent to the problem finder when observing the communication pattern. Some examples: Is there a proper match between the interaction capabilities of employees and job interaction requirements? Has the design of the job explicitly considered the interaction patterns that facilitate performance? Does the actual design of the job coincide with interaction requirements? Are job interaction requirements abetted or hindered by such peripheral arrangements as the chain of command (with its resultant rank and status), work flow arrangements, and physical job location? Do employees behave in the way that is expected of them?

The efficacy of the communication attempt itself is an equally important dimension when observing communication patterns. When managers communicate with each other or with subordinates they attempt to transplant their idea into the mind of the receiver. The process involves the act of putting the idea into symbols, transmitting the symbols, receiving the symbols on the part of the receiver, interpreting the symbols, verifying the message by providing feedback to the sender, accepting feedback from the receiver, and reiterating the cycle when necessary. The aim of the process is to achieve a match between the sender's idea and the receiver's ultimate idea. This ideal state does not usually occur. A number of hindrances exist. A sample of some of the common obstacles is suggested here to guide the problem finder in his task:

THE SENDER

- Translating the idea into inappropriate words, mannerisms, facial expressions, posture, eye contact, physical movements, tone, speed, or pitch
- Communicating on the basis of a stereotyped image of the receiver
- Failing to recognize the various meanings associated with words
- Engaging in a paradox of words and expressions—i.e., using inconsistent symbols
- Using an inappropriate media for transmitting the message
- Allowing interference from one's own preoccupations
- Failing to recognize that the situation adds overtones—time, place, principals involved, positions of authority
- Failing to see that people tend to see their situation in

highly personal terms—no two will see the world exactly alike
- Assuming that one will be understood
- Attempting to impress others
- Failing to receive feedback
- Engaging in some strategy—this may lead to a credibility gap

THE RECEIVER

- Allowing interference from receiver's preoccupations
- Engaging in defensive behavior that prevents real listening
- Failing to listen to the intended message
- Being unduly concerned with peripheral factors
- Interpreting symbols on the basis of the receiver's frame of reference
- Failing to recognize that people tend to interpret events in terms of their own most unsatisfied needs
- Providing a feedback overload
- Failing to sense when the sender is not ready for feedback

WORK FLOW

Some managers have expressed the idea that there is no substitute for a periodic personal observation of plant operations. The judicious use of this technique is effective since it concerns itself with where the action is—i.e., the grass-roots level of organization activity. For the problem finder, such an adventure may produce clues that lead to inappropriate tactical decisions governing day-to-day operations—for example, work procedures and work methods, work sequences, machine loadings, the order in which jobs are to be processed, work schedules, work loads, production lot size, or work assignments.

Work-flow observations are actually one of the prime responsibilities of supervisors. They are expected to communicate to their superiors the first telltale signs of a breakdown in the effectiveness of tactical decisions. Such observations can provide the problem finder with the kinds of clues that will help isolate inadequacies in the tactical decision area.

BUSINESS FUNCTIONS

Work-flow decisions govern all business functions. The problem finder may want to separate business functions into (1) those responsible for the availability of appropriate resources in the right type and the correct quantity, and (2) those that primarily utilize resources. The latter are usually referred to as line functions, while the resource-related functions are considered as staff functions.[4]

Line functions under this taxonomy include (1) production, (2) logistics, (3) marketing, and (4) (product) research and development; resource functions include (1) finance, (2) personnel, (3) purchasing, (4) accounting, and (5) (technology) research and development. Such subsidiary technical or professional activities as engineering, law, data processing, insurance, and advertising are included under one of the more basic functions they serve. The point of all this is that such a classification system serves to divide the total organization into distinct areas, each with its unique governing decisions. This should facilitate analysis.

BEHAVIORAL PATTERNS

Certain persistent behavioral patterns can readily be observed in the daily activity-interactions of people at work. Such an exercise is often used to infer motives from a person's behavior, but this should be done with considerable care. It is rather easy to be misled, and rarely does the manager have the time or the training to make a reasonable, thorough, and accurate assessment. However, management literature is re-

---

4. Finance is normally viewed as a line function due to its critical importance, although in reality it is a resource-oriented function. There is no real consensus as to the proper use of the term *staff*. Some feel it is an authority-related concept, while others use it to describe work responsibilities. Here it is used in the latter manner.

plete with the behavioral approach, and most management training programs spend considerable time on the psychology of human relations. It therefore seems appropriate to briefly review for the benefit of the problem finder two of the most common kinds of observations dealing with the psychology of people at work.

The behavioral patterns to be reviewed are interrelated, but, for the sake of clearer exposition, they will be treated as if unrelated. The first concerns psychological defense mechanisms. Most persons rely on such defenses to some extent to protect themselves psychologically from situations with which they cannot as yet cope. However, when such retreats become habitual in order to avoid the reality of a situation, then a necessary psychological "life preserver" is probably being used to the detriment of the organization as well as the individual.

Samples of some of the more prevalent mechanisms include:

- Compensation. When incapable or weak in some area, one compensates by becoming a perfectionist in another. The negative aspect arises when the perfection becomes an obsession and organizational requirements do not coincide with such behavior.
- Projection. This takes place when one assigns personal feelings to another. The negative aspect occurs when a persistent negative feeling is taken out on another in the organization, causing performance to suffer.
- Repression. When one puts an event or situation out of one's conscious mind, it is repressed. The negative aspect occurs when managers fail to face up to a situation so that organizational health begins to suffer.
- Identification. This mechanism operates when one identifies with or imitates someone or something. All leadership styles, as discussed earlier, tend to identify with a particular unit of the organizational system. The negative aspect, however, occurs when one identifies with individuals or groups whose aims run contrary to those of the organization.

The second set of behavioral patterns to be discussed comprises the interpersonal response traits, those recurring personality characteristics that are so valuable in the correct situation but so disruptive in other instances. For example, over time, the trained observer could construct for an individual a personality profile data bank that personality tests would probably be unable to match for reliability. What must be isolated are those traits that arise consistently over time. These traits can then be matched with jobs requiring certain distinctive traits. Of course, careful translation of job requirements into appropriate personal traits is a necessary adjunct for an effective match between job and employee.[5] Samples of such possible recurring traits include:

- Dependency (other directed) vs. independency (self-directed)
- Sociability (friendliness) vs. unsociability (unfriendliness)
- Agressiveness vs. nonaggressiveness
- Emotion vs. logic
- Domination vs. submission
- Sympathy vs. antipathy
- Competitiveness vs. noncompetitiveness
- Acceptance of others vs. rejection of others
- Social initiative vs. social passivity

When certain inappropriate interpersonal responses tend to persist, it is possible either that the individual or the group is "out of order" or that management's mode of operations has stimulated the response pattern. Perhaps both have contributed to the state of affairs. It is also possible that an individual's behavior has rational and logical origins that are quite di-

---

5. It is the position of this book that people have various talents and that most of the listed traits have value when directed into useful channels. The point is that organizational positions exist that could utilize most of the traits. This then becomes the challenge for management: to relate capability with organizational needs.

vorced from what management may or may not have done. The same commentary would apply to the defense mechanisms. The point is that inappropriate behavioral patterns are important clues, and their cause may have to be determined when the problem finder sees a reasonable relationship between the behavior and the significant deviations in organizational performance.

ADHERENCE TO POLICIES AND REGULATIONS

The propensity of people to behave in one way or another that is contrary to the rules and policies of an organization is a well-documented phenomenon. On the other hand, slavish adherence to rules when common sense dictates otherwise can be equally disruptive. However, when behaviors are obviously contrary to stated policy and extenuating circumstances do not justify a circumvention, then the problem finder will want to become aware of such situations. For example, during the past decade a number of abuses of corporate policy were uncovered causing considerable embarrassment and cost to the corporation. Such departures as price fixing and bribery should have been picked up at a much earlier date, but this may not always be an easy assignment to fulfill.

SUPERVISION

Even when the general style of supervision is appropriate, actions taken by a supervisor in individual cases may be inappropriate. In this category of activity-interaction analysis, the problem finder becomes interested in the behavior of supervisors where style is not in question. For example, Has Supervisor Bill Jones tended to his duties? Have his technical decisions reflected competence? Is he a capable trainer? Does he submit reports on time? Does he advise management of problems that arise and that are beyond his area of authority? It is just these kinds of actions that will sooner or later contribute significantly to performance competence or deficiency.

Overview of Activity-Interaction Phase

The activity-interaction cell is the source of important clues as to the causes of performance deficiencies. The problem finder here has the opportunity to observe a series of phenomena that may lead to possible management deficiencies:

- Are employees really exerting themselves? (degree of motivation)
- How smoothly is the work flow progressing? (work-flow pattern)
- Are employees overly defensive? (psychological defense mechanisms)
- Are recurring interpersonal response traits appropriate to the job? (personality traits)
- Does the style of leadership intertwine with situational requirements? (leadership style)
- Is the communicative work style of employees appropriate to job requirements? (communication patterns)
- Is the intended message received? (effective communication)
- Are activities and behaviors in accord with organizational intent? (adherence to policies)
- Are supervisors tending to their work responsibilities? (supervision)

Phase Three—Resource Analysis

Phase three of problem finding attempts to identify inadequacies in resources that occurred during the period in which performance deficiencies occurred. These inadequacies in resources may concern (1) the appropriate quantity, (2) the proper quality, (3) the appropriate type, or (4) the appropriate time. Generally, five categories of resources may be involved: (1) human resources, (2) physical assets, (3) financial resources, (4) technology, and (5) informational resources. For example, there may be a shortage of working capital at the end of the month, or a shortage of EDP-trained technicians for the evening shift.

Who is responsible for resource-related problems? How should the problem finder attempt to find the cause for resource deficiencies?

Resource deficiencies are produced by distinguishable subsystems of an organization. As an aid to analysis, resource-oriented activities can be viewed as involving (1) acquisition, (2) maintenance and compensation, (3) training and development, and (4) retirement activities.[6] Each of these activities can be viewed as a unique system with its distinctive results, activity-interaction, resources, and decisions or influences. Resource deficiencies can then be viewed as unsatisfactory results of a resource-oriented business function, for example, acquisition or development. A problem finder who becomes aware of a resource deficiency has in essence uncovered another significant deviation while seeking clues to explain a previously identified deviation. The analysis of the resource-related deviation will proceed in the same way as, for example, the analysis of a significant deviation in production or marketing. Of course, resource-related functions may be independently analyzed for significant deviations in the results analysis phase, as an open option of the problem finder; i.e., it is not necessary to refer to another function in which a resource problem has been identified.[7]

---

6. Acquisition involves those actions that are necessary to gain access to resources: buy, make, lease, borrow, or hire.

Maintenance and compensation activities involve those actions that are necessary to retain the resources or to maintain them at their required level of capability—e.g., physical maintenance of equipment, safety of the employees, insurance on plant and equipment, wage payments, fringe benefits, or credit policy.

Training and development involve actions intended to tap a resource's ability as well as its innate capacities—for example, management development programs, on-the-job training, investments, or trading on the equity.

Retirement involves activities for cancelling the organization's access to resources—for example, scrapping, sale, retirement, or firing.

7. Resource functions are not necessarily assigned to a specialized depart-

Phase Four—Reconstructing the Environmental Profile

The nature of environmental opportunities, threats, obstacles, or constraints during the period under review is one of the most crucial areas with which the problem finder must become familiar. Responses to the market, to competitors, to regulation play a major role in an organization's effectiveness or demise. Prior to the beginning of a fiscal period, certain assumptions about the environment will probably have been made, either explicitly or implicitly, and decisions taken with respect to such premises. Now, however, problem finding, after the fact, is concerned with reconstructing the actual environmental conditions that existed during the period under review, in order to determine whether the organization's responses were in line with actual conditions. For example, a company experiences a severe decline in sales. It was assumed that competitive forces would remain stable. On the basis of this assumption, the organization chose a pricing strategy based in large part upon limited competition. During the ensuing period several competitors moved into the company's market area with a lower price structure. Obviously, the pricing strategy was inappropriate in view of actual circumstances, and this would appear as the causal factor for the sales decline, other things being equal.

Phase five, decision and influence analysis, is the process in which significant deviations, activity-interaction clues, resource inadequacy clues, and environmental conditions are correlated with decisions and influences operating during the review period in order to arrive at causes—that is, the "real"

---

ment, but may be assigned to a line manager. For example, training may be performed either by the personnel department or the foreman on the job; hiring, by the line manager, by personnel, or by both. Specialized departments can perform the major portion of resource-related tasks, but irrespective of who carries on the resource activities, they require separate analysis by the problem finder. Ultimately, the problem finder may find it necessary to investigate both line and resource functions in order to cover all possible clue or causal areas.

problems. Before we proceed to this last phase, it must be noted that the process of relating significant deviations and clues to decisions that produced these events may be done concurrently with activity interaction, resource, or environmental analysis; that is to say, it is unnecessary to await phase five. Decision and influence analysis is distinguished as phase five largely for expository reasons. Its implementation can and probably should be carried on throughout the problem-finding process.

Phase Five—Decision and Influence Analysis

Phase five, decision and influence analysis, is a difficult one since it delves into the very essence of management itself. The purpose of this phase is to identify the relationship between decisions and extraorganizational influences on the one hand, and the clues or the significant deviations that have been previously discovered. Recall that clues include:

- Resource deficiencies
- Inappropriate behaviors and activities
- Environmental assumptions that failed to materialize
- Actual environmental conditions that did not mesh with the corporate mode of operation

Identifying the inappropriate decisions is analogous to identifying the causes. This implies that an essential prerequisite for effective problem finding is an understanding of the kinds of decisions managers make, their appropriateness to a situation, and the nature and effect of other influences in the management of an organization.

The "other" influences—i.e., the extraorganizational influences—exist side by side with the formal decisions and often contribute to a divergence from performance targets. They may exist in the form of personal goals and aspirations held by employees individually or as norms developed by informal groups. These groups always seem to arise spontaneously in organizations.

Decisions and the extraorganizational influences as governors of operations may be distinguished in this way: decisions represent the organization's formal attempts to influence or manage its environment and its resource capabilities; the extraorganizational influences represent forces that the formal decisions did not or could not direct or control. They, in effect, are residual forces that did not respond to the organization's influence attempts. As such they also exert influence in determining organization performance. For example, motivation programs are intended to challenge and channel employees' efforts toward organization goals. These programs obviously are never a complete success. Employees may balk when they do not see the relationship between management's efforts and their own ambitions or goals. When these goals run counter to organizational goals, they become one of the extraorganizational influences that must be reckoned with. Note, however, that the organization's attempt to motivate may have precipitated the negative reactions. For example, work standards may become a threat, and so groups establish output norms; relationships may appear unfair, and so employees diminish their efforts in order to compensate for what they see as an inequity.

An understanding of the origins and sources of employee or informal-group goals is a separate study, related to psychology and social psychology and beyond the scope of this book. Their relevance to the problem finder, however, is absolute. Such insights facilitate the problem finder's understanding of the governance systems of individuals and small groups and so improve problem-solving responses. For example, needs, desires, values, beliefs, attitudes, and experiences play critical roles in determining personal goals. These also change with time. At this point in the problem-finding process, it will suffice that the existence of personal and group goals as potential influencers of performance is recognized. This knowledge may enable the problem finder to uncover decision deficiencies, or constraints over which management could have exercised some influence but failed.

The Formal Decisions

One way to categorize formal decisions is in terms of strategic plans, tactical plans, and control decisions. The strategic decisions represent the organization's response to the opportunities, constraints, obstacles, and threats posed by its environment, conditioned by the organization's perception of its resource capabilities. Such decisions concern objectives, external strategies, internal strategies and policies, the organizational structure, and resource allocation decisions.

There is little consensus as to what organization objectives should really include. Many of the ideas expressed can be of value. Five perspectives should be given consideration. First is a general expression of the market *need* that the organization wishes to serve. The second concerns the general *recipient group* to which organization output is intended. The third perspective comprises the *states* the organization is pursuing, such as profitability, growth, quality. Fourth is the *creed* by which it wishes to abide while carrying on its pursuit. And fifth is some designation of *priorities,* particularly with respect to the various states and to the various interest groups that will be affected by company activities and outputs.

The organization's external strategies define the basic way in which its objectives are to be achieved. They "practicalize," make operational, the broad statements of intents (objectives). For each objective—and there may be one for each interest group, such as consumers, employees, suppliers, owner, and community—there will be a strategy to point the way, an underlying approach, to implement the objective.

The internal strategies refer to the basic ways in which the various business functions will be conducted. So, production may be pursued on a mechanized, assembly-line approach; marketing, on a direct-to-consumer basis. These strategies therefore serve to implement the external strategies. Policies, however, serve to implement the internal strategies. So, marketing may decide to meet competitive prices; personnel, to hire on a three-month trial basis; purchasing, to give preference to local suppliers, and finance, to limit credit privileges to the industrial sector. The distinction between a strategy and a policy is not always easily made. Some writers use them interchangeably. Both, however, represent strategic decisions.

Organization structure defines the basic way in which the work, the activities, of the organization will be divided and the basic way in which its efforts will be integrated. The division of work may be on a business-function basis, i.e., specialization by function. Integration may be achieved by a centralized command function. Many methods of departmentalization of work and integration can be utilized, and situational circumstances are the major considerations in choosing the most appropriate structure.

Resource allocation specifies the level of support to be granted to each organizational unit. It is predicated, of course, on an initial study of resource needs and resource specifications.

The tactical decisions are an extension of the strategic decisions and further operationalize and interpret their intents. The tactical decisions concern such areas as work procedures and methods, work schedules, work loads, and work sequences. Work methods and procedures break down the basic operation into detailed steps for the operator to perform. Work schedules set time constraints. Work loads involve work assignment decisions. Work sequence relates to the order in which jobs are processed, the assignment of jobs to machines, or the order in which resources are used. Tactical decisions are largely short-run decisions when they are contrasted to the strategic decisions. Tactical decisions usually lend themselves to quantitative and often deterministic analysis and conclusions, while their strategic counterpart may be more qualitative in nature. Tactical decisions are often determined at a much lower level in the management hierarchy than the strategic and may be determined, in part, by the operators themselves when participative management is appropriate.

The control decisions are essential for training and development and to achieve accountability. The term *control* is often viewed rather negatively. Yet, control is an absolute necessity. It must exist. It may reside in the self-control of the employee himself or in externally imposed controls. Neither one by itself can achieve maximum effort or maximum results. When reasonable men and women work together in organized effort, the principle becomes operative that, the greater the self-control of an employee, the greater the possibility for some degree of freedom, when situational circumstances make this feasible. For example, in a highly mechanized production process, the degree of employee freedom is restricted by the nature of the operation. Many office positions, on the other hand, can provide opportunities for the expression of varying degrees of creativity.

Control decisions include the assignment of work responsibilities, delegation of authority, determination of work standards, work evaluations, and verification that work targets were appropriate. The assignment of work responsibilities designates the tasks for which an employee will be held accountable. Authority delegation provides the formal right to make decisions with respect to the work responsibilities. Varying degrees of authority delegation are possible. Work standards involve decisions about the yardsticks to measure work performance and the target range within which results are expected to occur. Such decisions in turn require knowledge of the states to be achieved. Work evaluation requires that actual work performance be compared with the work target and an appraisal made. Target verification requires that work targets be reviewed in order to determine if they are, in fact, appropriate—that is, whether the actual environmental conditions during the review period and the actual resource capabilities would justify the appropriateness of the work targets as originally established.

Critical Variables for Formulating Strategic Decisions

Objectives, external strategies, and internal strategies attempt to relate corporate resource capabilities with environmental circumstances while maintaining consistency within these strategic decisions. This is shown in Fig. 2.8.

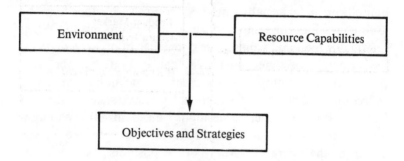

FIG. 2.8.   FACTORS IN FORMULATING STRATEGIC DECISIONS

The organization structure decision must consider (1) the state of the environment (i.e., its degree of stability, its rate of change, and its uniformity of change); (2) product and market characteristics (i.e., the size and degree of uniformity of the market and products); (3) characteristics of the technologies employed (i.e., their complexity, their reliability, the nature of the work flow); and (4) the priorities with respect to diverse state achievements (e.g., profitability, growth, social responsibility, efficiency); and the priorities with respect to interest groups (customers, owners, employees, suppliers, and community). Practically, personal variables (e.g., personal ambitions or goals) also are reflected in structural decisions and could be at odds with organization purpose. These ideas are diagrammed in Fig. 2.9.

Component Parts of Decisions—
The Strategic Design Decisions

In the ensuing pages a brief description of a very extensive body of research and administrative practices will be attempted. First, the strategic decisions.

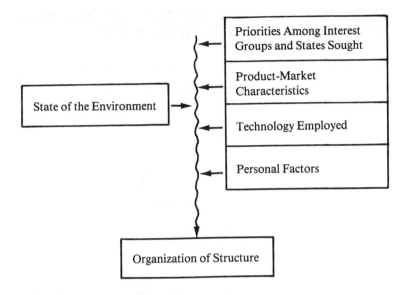

FIG. 2.9.   DETERMINANTS OF ORGANIZATIONAL
STRUCTURE

OBJECTIVES—THEIR COMPONENT PARTS

Needs. Probably one of the most important components of
setting objectives relates to designating a category of *needs*
in the market to which the organization will address itself.
The several need categories that exist can be specifically
identified by interest groups. The interest groups are those
who will be affected directly or indirectly through the activities or by the outputs of the organization. Customers, owners,
employees, suppliers, and the community are examples of such
interest groups. Objectives should be stated in terms of those
interest group needs that the organization hopes to meet. The
organization objective with respect to owners could state that
it is the company's intent to provide for an adequate return
on the owners' investment, or it may state that it is the com-

pany's intent to ensure a constant growth in the value of the owners' investment.

The objective with respect to the company's customers may state, for example, that the company intends to be in the business of providing for the transportation needs of its customers, or that the company is in the container business. An objective with respect to employees may state that it is the organization's intent to provide job security or personal achievement and growth opportunities. The "supplier" objective could indicate an intent to foster long-term and profitable relationships, and a "community" objective could seek to maintain a clean environment or to become an active participant in solving community problems. The common dimension of these objectives is that they are output oriented—i.e., they designate in broad terms the kind of things or opportunities the organization intends to provide.

Recipients. The second vital part of objectives relates to the recipients, the groups that are to be the market for or the receivers of organization outputs. The owners, employees, suppliers, and community are largely predetermined interest groups, but the customer designation will vary with the resource capabilities and the interests of the organization, provided that need exists. The corporate objective with respect to its customer group should provide a general designation of the market it intends to enter over the planning horizon—in the very long run. Broad geographical market segments or customer type may be designated. These decisions, in effect, determine the arena in which the organization will seek out opportunities. More specific designations and necessary refinements await strategy formulation, which considers shorter time intervals as its planning horizons. So, for example, if the "market" objective is the domestic large contract market, current "market" strategy could reflect a move into the federal government contract area when such an opportunity appears attractive, but may be quickly reversed if conditions change. The objective provides the broad focus—the large contract market; the strategy, the more specific group in the contract arena—federal government contract business.

States. The third aspect of objectives concerns the states the organization hopes to achieve. States are defined as the characteristics of the organization as a whole or some significant part of the organization. Profitability, efficiency, or effectiveness are common aims of business organization. Creativity is sought by some. Quality of service or product, flexibility in physical resources, adaptability to changing conditions may also be pursued. Others who place high value on human relations seek to be responsive to people's needs.

States are not always mutually exclusive. Responsiveness or adaptability may impinge on efficiency or profitability. Other conflicting states are evident. It is interesting to note that most decisions define a course of action that is directed to some state achievement; at the same time, however, costs are involved that become drawbacks to the attainment of other states. The trade-off becomes the key consideration. To pay over union scale may increase job satisfaction or, in Herzberg's terms, decrease job dissatisfaction (Herzberg), but higher pay may decrease creativity if the effect is to retain the employees who seek security and to lose those who desire job challenge.

To review, states indicate the "effect" the organization seeks from its decisions, its activities, its outputs. These effects involve corporate customers, other interest groups, and corporate resources. Needs designate the basic kinds of output, while market defines the kind or location of recipients.

Priorities. The fourth dimension of objectives concerns itself with designating priorities with respect to the multiple "state" objectives and diverse "interest group" objectives. Most decisions already carry an implicit priority designation, but an explicit priority designation—which tends to promote greater consistency among decisions and facilitates problem finding and problem solving—is often difficult to extract. Decision makers often hesitate to be put on record, and setting priorities is a trying and complex task, and priorities can change rapidly. Most problem finders and solvers can readily recall comments such as, "We've got to get our priorities sorted out," or "Let's face it, we all can pretty well sense what counts around here!" But getting "what counts" formalized is a difficult undertaking. It would be desirable to have a neat array of priorities that rarely change, but, unfortunately, this is an unrealistic hope. Priorities do change and often as rapidly as one moves from crisis to crisis. Nevertheless, setting priorities is a necessity, whether by thoughtful design or by default.

Creed. The final aspect of objectives declares the creed to which the organization wants to subscribe—that is, the kind of organization it wants to be while carrying on its activities. The subscription becomes a statement of the corporation's philosophy, the values it wants to reflect, the code of ethics it wishes to follow. Such a creed is intended as a sincere expression for the guidance of the organization's managers and employees.

EXTERNAL STRATEGIES—THEIR COMPONENT PARTS

External strategies express the basic way in which objectives are to be achieved. Formulating them is the first step for implementing the broad aims provided in the objectives. They define the need, the market, and the creed more specifically, but within the constraints of states and priorities. Product and market strategies represent the key decisions. The "customer" product-market strategy is concerned with product line, product mix, and market segment. Similarly, owner, supplier, community, and employee objectives require an expression of strategy.

Strategy formulation is based upon a process that meshes environmental circumstances with corporate resource capabilities. This implies that the significant and relevant environmental forces and the organization's resource potentials must be discovered.

The environment is the source of varying opportunities, constraints, obstacles, and threats. The critical variables involved in a choice of product strategy, for example, may be found by focusing on some of the following variables.

- Focus on the industry
  capital requirements, ease of entry
  growth or declining industry
  excess or insufficient capacity
  nature of its economies of scale
- Focus on competition
  number and size of competitors
  nature of the dominant competitive tool (price, product differentiation, style, quality, service)
- Focus on the buyers
  buying habits—seasonal, quantity
  channel of distribution—direct to consumer, wholesalers, etc.
  credit needs
  number and size of buyers
- Focus on the product
  availability of substitutes
  kind of product—industrial, consumer, susceptibility to disposable personal income (DPI), etc.
  nature of changes occurring in the product
- Focus on government aid and regulation
  regarding the product or service itself
  pricing
  promotion
  manufacturing
  taxes and financial restrictions
  employee relations
  economic and fiscal policy
- Focus on the unions
  the bargaining unit
  current demands
  union-management relations

- Focus on the social norms and demographic characteristics
  nature of consumerism
  population size and other pertinent characteristics
  ethical values
- Focus on the political climate
  liberal or conservative
  type of governmental system
- Focus on resource vendors
  size and number of suppliers
  location
  price and terms
- Focus on economic conditions
  inflation rate
  interest rate
  economic growth rate

Environmental variables should be identified in terms of their present value and their anticipated value over the planning period and applied to the organization in terms of their expected impact. Their application may reflect an opportunity, a constraint, an obstacle, or a threat. For example, the strategy of a competitor may be the instrument for providing an opportunity for another.

The nature of the organization's resource capabilities, including both strengths and weaknesses, currently available or available during the future planning horizon, must also be tabulated. For example:

- The state of its financial capacities, including credit rating, line of credit, etc.
- The state of its managerial capabilities—experience, age, etc.
- The state of the rank-and-file skill level
- The organization's technological know-how
- The state of its physical and intangible assets, including product image, location, dealers, branches, plant, equipment, materials

- The state of its informational resources—e.g., market data

The choice of strategy ultimately reflects the organization's personal response to its environment, conditioned by its perception of that environment and its own present and future capabilities. The perceived values of each significant and relevant environmental and resource factor become the organization's planning assumptions or premises. These premises should be explicitly stated for all who are or will become involved in their implementation.

INTERNAL STRATEGIES—THEIR COMPONENT PARTS

Internal strategies are those decisions that specify the basic way in which a business line or resource function is to be conducted. The choice of manufacturing technology and the choice between seasonal or year-round production are examples of manufacturing strategy. A choice of channel of distribution and a choice between a hard or soft sell are examples of marketing strategy. Choice of transport mode and inventory safety stock would relate to logistics strategy.

The various resource-oriented functions that deal with the acquisition, compensation, maintenance, development, and retirement of organization resources are also carried out under broad strategy statements. For example, it may be the strategy of an organization to generate funds internally, to be an equal opportunity employer, to engage in preventive maintenance of plant and equipment, to retire all management personnel at sixty-five, or to make all purchases that exceed $1,000 by competitive bids.

The formulation of internal strategies requires that due consideration be given to the organization objectives, external strategies, and budgetary constraints. Likewise, internal consistency among the various functional strategies must be maintained. For example, it would probably be a contradiction to choose a mass production technology where the marketing strategy is directed to catering to individual customers' needs.

ORGANIZATION STRUCTURE—ITS COMPONENT PARTS

Organization structure refers to the basic way in which the total work of the organization will be divided and how integration is to be achieved. Structure decisions, therefore, comprise two areas of concern:

- The division of work—the basic method of departmentalizing or specializing operations. Work may be divided, for example, by business function, by product, by location, or by the maturity of a product (i.e., distinguishing between established products and the untested product ventures).
- Integration—the basic method of achieving coordinated effort directed toward organizational purposes. Methods of integration include using higher authority, using those among the managerial ranks who are the most competent to judge, and using the competence of the grass roots— i.e., the operators themselves.

The two dimensions of organizational structure work in opposite directions in order to make possible the achievement of organization aims. Division of work divides the organization, while integration provides the means to bring it back together.

Factors to Be Considered in Deciding upon an Appropriate Structure. In the following few pages a brief outline of the determinants and aims of organization structure decisions will be attempted.

1. *Environmental States*
   - Rate of product-service obsolescence (static-dynamic)
   - Rate of technology obsolescence (slow-rapid)
   - Rate of change in product demand, competition, economic factors, political and social climate, availability of required resources (slow-rapid)
   - The uniformity of change for each of the above (uniform-diverse)

- The nature of short-run variations for each of the above (static-erratic)
- Availability and clarity of information (good-poor)

2. *Characteristics of the Product and Market*
   - Size of market (small-large)
   - Number of products (few-many)
   - Product variety (homogeneous-heterogeneous)
   - Market uniformity (similar-dissimilar)

3. *Characteristics of the Technologies Employed*
   - The complexity of the technology as measured by knowledge requirements (routine-complex)
   - The reliability of the technology (sure-unsure or few exceptions–many exceptions)
   - Work flow characteristics (continuous-noncontinuous)
   - Availability of feedback on results (short run–long run)
   - Perspectives among functional groups (similar-dissimilar)—e.g., in terms of time horizons and goals (states sought) (Lorsch and Lawrence)

4. *Priorities*
   - Of various states that are sought
   - Of various interest groups

The four elements—environment, product-market, technology, and priorities—all play a vital role in an appropriate choice of corporate structure. The suggested measure following each factor reflects the characteristics that are the important determiners. On the one hand, they reflect constancy (static, slow, uniform, small, few, homogeneous, similar, routine, sure, few exceptions, continuous, short run); on the other hand, they reflect variableness (dynamic, rapid, diverse, erratic, large, many, heterogeneous, complex, unsure, many exceptions, noncontinuous, long run). These are the kinds of things that differentiate situations, and it is these things that point to the need for unique structures to cope with unique situations.

Some Alternative Arrangements for the Division of Work. A wide array of structural arrangements has been tested and used. Some of the more basic structures will be discussed briefly below, but many variations, hybrids, and combinations are possible (Ansoff and Brandenburg).

1. Functional—i.e., by business function. Line-function specialization will usually occur early in the life of an organization; as the organization grows, staff specialization may be added—i.e., in the resource (service) groups such as personnel, purchasing, accounting, or legal. Later, managerial staff units may be split off to provide assistance in such managerial functions as planning or control.

The functional arrangement is usually conducive to the achievement of such states as efficiency and stability, and it is generally appropriate in environmental conditions in which constancy tends to predominate. Such an environment does not appear to pose any insurmountable problem for the functional form, which tends to be characterized by a slower and less flexible response to internal and external change. Management development under the functional arrangement also appears to be more difficult due to the emphasis upon specialization.

2. Divisional—i.e., by product or region; then by function. Almost inevitably as more and more growth occurs, divisional groupings become a necessity. The complexity associated with growth or with diversity of products, markets, technologies, and environments calls for regional or product specialization in order to maintain efficiency and to achieve greater responsiveness to changing conditions. Centralized as well as divisionalized staff may be added.

A transition to divisionalization is the product manager arrangement, which grants liaison responsibilities to that position. The profit center or cost center concept is often used in the divisionalized arrangement for control purposes. Opportunities for general management development are greater with divisional groupings than with functional groupings. Generally the divisional form is appropriate for product-market and environmental characteristics that reflect less constancy—that is, more likelihood of change in the critical variables.

3. Venture. The common aim of the venture arrangement is to foster flexibility and creativity while retaining the advantages of the divisional form. It represents a structural adaptation to growth and to the need for a highly responsive posture with respect to changes both without and within the firm. The venture arrangement splits off the new venture product from the established products in order to divorce the propensity for stability that is still an inherent feature of the divisional arrangement. Having a venture division allows for the retention of the profit or cost center concepts for the established products while avoiding the transfer of profit or cost pressures upon the new venture. The idea of ventures can be extended to programs or projects that are not necessarily associated with the diversified undertakings of a large organization. The key factor is that the situation is characterized by considerable variableness, so that the division of work cannot be by functional specialization, but must have a structure that is primarily product-output oriented. In a way, such a structure is analogous to the small corner grocery store of years ago in which employees worked at all sorts of jobs wherever they were needed or had the qualifications to contribute a needed perspective. The criterion was What can I contribute? rather than, Does this belong to my function?

Some Alternative Arrangements for Integration. Division of work is concerned with stipulating the work duties of employees. This definition may be rigid or loosely designated. Integration, on the other hand, is concerned with stipulating who is to determine what, how, when, and where the task is to be accomplished. In other words, the question becomes, Where does the authority lie? The answer may reflect a broad or narrow delegation; specific individuals, groups, or both may be granted this authority.

A great deal has been written about who should decide, the rights of individuals to decide, the motivational impact of possessing the right to decide, or the organizational benefits that accrue by delegating the authority to decide. The scientific rigor that characterizes some of the research in participative management is on occasions rather questionable. For example, when it is possible to use identical data generated by an experiment and then to arrive at diametrically opposite conclusions, then the credibility gap begins to widen. Value judgments tend to abound, and often they are not identified as assumptions that underlie the conclusions (Lee). The tendency to follow what appears to be popular, politically expedient, or something new seems to characterize many research efforts. Where then can the problem finder look for guidance when there exists such a wide range of suggested paths to apparently greater achievements?

The answers to the dilemma are not easy. Ultimately one must discover the priorities and values in which the organization believes. In many instances the priority exists in providing the product or service that the market demands or needs. The criteria for integration decisions then arise out of the nature of the task, and they should provide the necessary guidance as to where and with whom authority is to be placed. The whims and desires of individuals have no immediate value. Ultimately, however, it is the capabilities of the individuals, the knowledge they possess, the information they generate, and the judgment they show that become the key considerations in making delegation decisions. Three alternative integration methods are discussed below.

1. Hierarchical Authority. At various levels in the hierarchy, formal decision-making authority is granted to specific individuals, who then possess the formal right to command. The underlying assumption is that, at the established decision-making point, the decision maker knows best, has the information, is capable of understanding the data, and appreciates the trade-offs involved.

2. Competence. The assumption here is that formal hierarchical authority and technical or managerial competence in complexity cannot always coexist. Capacities for competence exist in one who has the technical skills or who can

capture the ramifications of varying costs and varying benefits associated with alternative courses of action. Ideally, formal authority voluntarily tempered by competence inputs
from others would generally achieve optimum integration.
Theoretically, the line and staff concept is based on this notion, but human frailties cause innumerable conflicts. Research
findings suggest that, when formal decision makers face up
to the issues and conflicts involved and secure the contributions of all those who are affected, the organization's end
performance is often improved (Walker and Lorsch).

Generally, the unit primarily responsible for a particular
"state" attainment is placed at the focal point around which
integration is achieved (Dalton, Lawrence, and Lorsch). For
example, when quality has high priority, the production function is the unit best fitted to coordinate the efforts of marketing and R&D. Or, when employee relations become a key
priority issue, whether on principle or by necessity, the industrial labor relations department may be placed at a higher
level in the hierarchy commensurate with its needed inputs
into the organizational decision-making machinery.

3. Grass Roots. The grass-roots method is actually a subset of the competence approach but focuses on a specific level
at which integration can be achieved. Here the assumption is
made that coordination is best achieved when the employees
who carry out the operations are also in charge of making
the required decisions. The area of discretion is confined to
actions that do not infringe upon or affect other groups and
to decisions that the grass-roots participants qualify as the
most competent to make.

An interesting situation exists with the two aspects of corporate structure—division of work and integrating mechanisms. The greater the specialization, the greater the need for
integrating mechanisms. Specialization produces economies,
but integration efforts are costly. Here again an appropriate
balance must be sought.

Some States That Structure Can Effect. Structure can influence state achievement by some of the methods illustrated below.

- Efficiency
  through specialization
  by splitting off decision making from those who perform the operations
- Stability
  by centralizing authority
  by increasing the number of management levels
- Flexibility
  by putting decision-making authority close to where the action or the relevant information resides
- Creativeness
  through product grouping or regional grouping
  by decentralizing authority
  by splitting off new products from established products
  by distinguishing planning and development from implementation and operations
- Awareness
  through open communication channels
  through liaison personnel
- Accountability
  by clear assignment of work and authority
  through profit or cost centers
  through an appropriate balance between work responsibilities and decision authority

The particular structural devices suggested do not automatically produce the associated state. Structural devices only facilitate state achievement.

Some Symptoms of Inappropriate Structural Arrangements. A sample of possible significant deviations, inappropriate behaviors, or resource deficiencies is provided below to illustrate some of the manifestations of inappropriate structural arrangements.

- Drop in market share due to structural rigidities that unduly inhibit timely response to change
- Undue stockouts due to an inability to respond to increased demand brought about by delays in decision making
- Reduced efficiency due to technological obsolescence and delayed response to such change
- Inability to identify where responsibility rests
- Ignorance of what is really happening
- Too many people doing their "own thing"
- Continual loss of "good" ideas in the maze of red tape

RESOURCE ALLOCATION—ITS COMPONENT PARTS

In resource allocation decisions, the budgeting process, several prior determinations must be made before a budget is adopted. For example, resource needs for a program must be ascertained, resource specifications provided, and the level of support to be granted the program must be determined. Concurrently, available resources must be inventoried, particularly the financial capabilities of the organization, before a fiscal resource allocation can be committed to a given program.

Component Parts of Decisions—Control Decisions

The control decisions, according to the taxonomy used here, involve not only the evaluations of performance, but prior decisions upon which evaluations must be based. These would include the assignment of work to specific individuals, the delegation of authority, the determination of standards to measure performance, and finally the evaluation itself.

WORK ASSIGNMENT—ITS COMPONENT PARTS

After the basic structural arrangement has been determined, the task begins of making specific work responsibility assignments, usually formalized in the form of job descriptions. Considerations with respect to the formal requirements of the job and with respect to the human element are factors that warrant special attention.

Conditions to Be Fostered—Formal Job Requirements. Work assignment decisions should be based upon criteria reflecting formal job requirements. For example:

- Providing adequate control—splitting a function to ensure adequate control (dividing receiving from the disbursement of funds)
- Creating competition—assigning similar work responsibilities to several individuals in order to create a basis for competitive activity
- Securing competent handling—assigning specific work aspects to those who possess the ability to handle them or express an interest

States Sought—The Human Dimension. Work assignment decisions should also be based upon criteria for achieving human job satisfactions when this is at all feasible. The benefits will usually accrue under a longer-run perspective—i.e., beyond the immediate short run. Such considerations are usually manifestations of enlightened management. For example:

- Security—avoidance of work assignments that are beyond the employees' capacities in order to avoid personal failure
- Growth—assignment of work that provides challenge and opportunity to learn and to develop one's capabilities
- Satisfaction—assign work that is intrinsically interesting; avoid the too narrow specialization (job enlargement)

AUTHORITY DELEGATION—ITS COMPONENT PARTS

Following the specific work assignments, there emerges the need for delegating authority. The former identifies what is to be done; the latter extends to the employee the formal area of discretion that may be exercised by him or her in doing the job. The one without the other would result in stagnation.

Authority delegation also possesses two perspectives for consideration: the formal job requirements and the human dimension.

Conditions to Be Fostered—Formal Job Requirements. The formal job requirements as a rule must take precedence in deciding upon the delegation of authority. Authority delegation decisions should, therefore, be based upon criteria reflecting such requirements. For example:

- Accountability

    to attain as close a balance between work responsibilities and decision-making authority as is consistent with the overall circumstances of the situation

- Coordination

    to ensure that authority is granted to the position that can best effect needed coordination, provided that this will mesh with overall corporate aims

States Sought—The Human Dimension. Opportunities for human need satisfaction also arise through grants of job authority. These formal rights to manage one's own job (they often will mean the right to command others) are becoming increasingly important for a growing segment of employees. Commensurate with the employees' abilities, often latent, tapping these wants can provide many opportunities for need satisfaction. Doing so can redound to the organization's welfare through highly motivated people. (Argyris; Donnelly; Herzberg; Likert; Maslow; McGregor). Examples of need satisfaction opportunities may include:

- Personal growth—management capabilities can ultimately be learned only through exercising supervisory, command, or leadership positions

- Self-confidence and esteem—the opportunity provided through delegation may lead to challenge and then achievement

WORK STANDARDS—THEIR COMPONENT PARTS

The criteria against which work performance is to be evalu-

ated can be developed with reference to the following factors:
- States to be achieved
- Yardsticks to measure state achievement
- Resource capabilities
- Situational circumstances
- Target range

These factors and the process of setting targets were covered in an earlier section of this chapter. The critical point here is that a target against which an employee's performance will be evaluated must take into consideration the realities of the situation and the employee's capabilities. The targets themselves must arise out of appropriate devices to measure the states to be achieved.

WORK EVALUATIONS—THEIR COMPONENT PARTS

Work evaluation represents the final consummation of the preceding control decisions and involves the following steps:
- Securing information on work results
- Comparing performance with the target range
- Determining the significance of any negative deviations
- Checking on the appropriateness of the target range

The work evaluation process was described in some detail in an earlier section of this chapter. The result of this activity, identifying significant deviations, then becomes the impetus for problem-finding activity to commence.

Component Parts of Decisions—The Tactical Decisions

The tactical decisions concern work procedure and work methods, work schedules, work sequences, and work loads. Their content varies with the particular business function under consideration. Some of these decisions change on a day-to-day basis; others remain viable for much longer periods of time. They are usually technical in nature. No attempt will be made to cover the nature of tactical decisions with respect to production, finance, marketing, personnel, logistics, or other functional areas. Although problem-finding processes are suitable for isolating specific functional management deficiencies at the tactical level, the problem finder at higher levels of management will want to proceed beyond the tactical deficiencies whenever more basic causes appear to be operating.

Determining Linkages between Decisions and Results

It is no easy task to discover the "real" causal connectors to significant deviations. The methodology has taken the problem finder in stepwise fashion from significant deviations to inappropriate targets, inappropriate behaviors, resource deficiencies, and inappropriate assumptions and premises about the environment. As this evidence has surfaced, inquiries as to its cause should probably have led the problem finder to discover some inappropriate decisions. At times, however, the causes may be subtle and difficult to identify, and so the line of inquiry could take another approach. Some of the following questions might be particularly discerning:

- Did decisions mesh with actual conditions (market, resource capabilities, activities, other decisions)?
- Were decisions fully and adequately implemented?
- Were decisions really communicated and understood?

A full review of decision types and their constituent parts, as covered in this chapter, could also serve as an additional checkpoint.

Finally, a quick review of the kinds of linkages that researchers have identified in the past may be helpful (Price). The list in Table 2.4 is incomplete, but it does illustrate the most common relationships between variables.

In the table, linkage I-A reflects that low wages without the assistance of any other force results in high employee turnover. The condition of low wages is *sufficient* for the effect. On the other hand, Linkage I-B suggests that a drop in market share is caused by high prices, but only if a soft-sell approach

TABLE 2.4.   LINKAGES BETWEEN DECISIONS AND RESULTS

Example	Type
If low wages: high employee turnover	I-A
If high price: drop in market share; only if use soft-sell approach	I-B
If a retrenchment, and only if a retrenchment: drop in absenteeism	II-A
If inferior raw material: rise in production costs; but if tight standards, also rise in production costs	II-B
If close supervision: few product defects; and if few product defects: close supervision	III-A
If employee-oriented leadership style: high morale; but if high morale: unable to identify with leadership style	III-B
If high job specialization: probably low morale	IV-A
If poor delivery service policy: always lost customers	IV-B
If poor maintenance program: then later high equipment downtime	V-A
If high interest rates: then also drop in customer inquiries	V-B
If drop in price: increase in sales	VI-A
If heavy customer demand: high employee absenteeism	VI-B

is coupled with high price. High price thus can produce a drop in market share, but this is *contingent* upon the use of the soft-sell approach.

Other linkages are grouped in pairs in which the one stands in contrast to the other. More specifically, the second group represents a *necessary* vs. a *substitution*-type relationship; the third group, *reversible* vs. *irreversible;* the fourth group, *random* vs. *deterministic*; the fifth group, *sequential* vs. *coextensive;* and the sixth group, *causal* vs. *illusory*—an accidental parallelism.

In organizational analysis, the relationships will rarely be simple. Many variables operate simultaneously. Probably the most common relationship will be of the contingent type, random, sequential, irreversible, and substitutionary. The others, reversible, necessary, sufficient, deterministic, coextensive, real, and illusory certainly exist, but they are more difficult to positively relate to actual experiences. In other words, judgment plays a critical role in problem finding. Situations are different. The nagging feeling persists that perhaps some important facet of a situation has been overlooked, deemphasized, or ignored. It is the aim of this problem-finding methodology, however, to minimize, at least, the feeling that important variables may have been overlooked.

Constructing a Hierarchy of Decisions

The aim of problem finding is to identify the most basic causes over which the decision maker has discretionary authority to make changes. This may mean that a series of interrelated decisions must be identified. Problem finders will experience considerable help in this process by using some of the following aids:

- One of the most effective devices is to ask at each stage of the problem-finding process the simple question, Why? If resources are inadequate—Why? When schedules are inappropriate—Why? The purpose: Find the most basic decision that relates to a clue.
- Many decisions can be conceived of as implementations of other decisions. The ultimate cause for poor performance may rest with a decision that preceded the implementation. For example, work standards may be inappropriate as a result of an unrealistic decentralization strategy.
- Decisions must be implemented. A common cause for new program failures is the absence of effective and complete implementing actions. In these cases, the problem finder must discover an absence of action rather than an inappropriate action.

Selling the Problem-Finding Analysis

Convincing the appropriate management level that certain decisions hold the key to performance improvement will usually require a well-planned effort. Dogmatic assertions that

Decision X caused Result Y are rarely successful, and, even if they are accepted, there is a very high probability that there will be little consensus as to why this relationship holds. There are several ways to avoid misunderstandings of this kind or failures to convince management that the problem finder's analysis is worthy of serious consideration.

- Illustrating relationships discovered by scientific research. However, making sure that the organization's situation is reasonably similar to that of the research upon which reliance is placed.
- Justifying an assertion by putting it in the context of the organization's environment and its resource capabilities.
- Using sound deductive logic—i.e., moving from the general (the decision deemed inappropriate) to the specific (the significant deviation).
- Having done your homework—i.e., having carefully considered the full spectrum of significant results and causes as suggested by the problem-finding methodology.

Problem Finding as a Group Effort

Up to now, the problem-finding process has largely been described as if it were a one-man affair. This is not necessarily the case. A growing body of literature based upon both speculation and sound research is available; it focuses on a group approach to problem identification and problem solving. Unfortunately, too often the group approach has been sold as a panacea rather than a selective application. It is critical to recognize, in this regard, that the vehicle that should be used for problem finding depends upon the kind of situation facing the firm. The analysis provided for leadership styles can also be applied to problem finding. There are times when one person can best handle the process, there are situations that require considerable consultation on a one-to-one basis, and there are instances in which a group orientation is essential.

SOME REALITIES OF HUMAN NATURE
AND THE PROBLEM-FINDING PROCESS

Time and time again, as one picks up management texts or articles or listens to the practitioners in the field, a recurring theme seems to come through, explicitly or implicitly. "Our biggest problem is with people." And this has equal application with problem-finding procedures. It is a fact of life that many managers and workers speak more frankly and more honestly when they can remain anonymous, when they are not forced into a position of personally embarrassing a colleague or a supervisor, or when they are not forced to publicly suggest ideas about which they are unsure of support. The increased complexity of many problem-finding situations today results in more instances in which group problem finding must be used. The pressure of the "democratic ethic" further reinforces this need.

Groups are usually composed of individuals who tend to dominate and those who submit; those who assert themselves and those who wait to be asked; those who speak freely and those who experience considerable difficulty in speaking out; those who have little to contribute of substance and those who have a maximum contribution to make.

In a group problem-finding situation, conditions may be created whereby individuals will be motivated to contribute or inhibited from contributing. Group processes are complicated when the purpose for which the group is assembled is to find the problem. Since the problem is usually associated with or can involve people, all kinds of defensive maneuvering—which is anathema to scientific problem finding—are precipitated.

The manner in which the group is structured can maximize or minimize the self-defeating tendencies of such groups in a problem-finding exercise. One such structure will be briefly reviewed below in order to illustrate that groups, if appropriately designed, and if used in an appropriate situation, can be a key variable in problem-finding effectiveness.

THE SILENT-INTERACTING GROUP

No one technique can overcome all problems implicit in people problems. The silent-interacting group approach may, however, produce more benefits than costs. It is worthy of experiment. Used in the correct situation and where time is not of the essence, it may well produce some startling insights.

The process is rather simple:

1. The problem must require the insight and contributions of a number of people.
2. Group members assemble physically and interact through written memos about causes as they see them.
3. The memos are collected by a trusted outsider (i.e., not a member of the group). The ideas are sorted, printed, and distributed to the group. The authors, of course, remain anonymous.
4. Participants react to any or all ideas as they see fit. Frankness and openness are encouraged.
5. Reactions are collected, duplicated, and returned to all members of the group, anonymously.
6. Responses to reactions are made by participants, picked up, duplicated, and returned to participants.
7. The role of the outsider is crucial. Consensus must be gleaned from responses. Areas of wide differences must be recognized. Periodic summaries should be provided for the group, indicating where consensus appears and where differences remain. In the event of obvious omissions, suggested areas for consideration could be included in the summary. In no way should the outsider take a position of leadership in the normal meaning of the word. The group must be the focal point that originates ideas and judges their worthiness.

The silent-interacting group is a close adaptation of the nominal decision-making process suggested by Van de Ven. Variant structures exist, and most problem-finding situations using group processes should readily fit into one of these without major changes. For example, ideas may be expressed orally and recorded on a flip chart without comment or evaluation until all ideas have been placed before the group (Van de Ven and Delbecq; Van de Ven).

Charting Aids for Operations Analysis

Numerous charting aids have been prepared to assist the problem-finding process. Data sheets have been prepared for each phase of problem finding.

- Data Sheet for Results Analysis, After the Fact—Table 2.5
- Data Sheet for Activity-Interaction Analysis—Table 2.7
- Data Sheet for After-the-Fact Resource Capabilities Analysis—Table 2.8
- Data Sheet for Developing an After-the-fact Environmental Profile—Table 2.10
- Decision and Influence Checklist—Table 2.12
- After-the-Fact Resumé Sheet—Table 2.13

DATA SHEET FOR RESULTS ANALYSIS, AFTER THE FACT

The Data Sheet for Results Analysis, After the Fact (Table 2.5) may be used as a work sheet for recording data relative to results. The first column identifies the result category that is to be investigated. The category identifies the unit of analysis—for example, the organization as a whole, products, regional groupings, or business functions. Any one or all may be relevant to a problem. At the organization level, results with respect to customers, owners, employees, suppliers, or the community may be meaningful. Results data for organizations with diverse products or locations should preferably be separated by product line or by regional groupings. Ultimately results with respect to distinct business functions will probably be necessary.

The second column provides space for identifying the states that were sought with respect to the unit of analysis.

The third column provides space to record the measure that

TABLE 2.5.   DATA SHEET FOR RESULTS ANALYSIS,
AFTER THE FACT

(1) Result Category	(2) State Sought	(3) Measure	(4) Target	(5) Actual Result	(6) Significant Deviation	(7) Result Index
Examples:						
Organization	Profit-ability	ROI	10-14%	8%	2% off from minimum target	Profit
Production	Effi-ciency	Cost per unit	75-80¢	83¢	3¢ off from maximum target	Cost

is used for evaluating state achievement. For example, marketing effectiveness could be measured by sales volume, complaints received, or returned sales. The concept of countermeasures to avoid suboptimization becomes an issue at this point—for example, sales volume needs a profit constraint.

The fourth column is used to record the target or standard against which performance will be evaluated. These columns, in effect, summarize the charters of accountability, pinpoint responsibilities, or reflect the management-by-objectives perspective.

The fifth column provides space for noting actual performance.

The sixth column provides space for recording significant deviations from target.

The last column is to be used as a reference index for each entry on the results data sheet. This provides the means by which entries on the various data sheets can be cross-

TABLE 2.6. SELECTED RATIOS FOR ORGANIZATIONAL ANALYSIS

THE STATE THAT IS MEASURED	THE RATIO	SOME EXPLANATORY COMMENTS
Liquidity	$\dfrac{\text{Current Assets}}{\text{Current Liabilities}}$	Known as the current ratio. A measure of the ability to meet short-term obligations.
	$\dfrac{\text{Current Assets Less Inventories}}{\text{Current Liabilities}}$	Known as the quick ratio. Eliminates the inventory variable, which could include dead, obsolete, or slow-moving items.
	$\dfrac{\text{Inventories}}{\text{Current Assets Less Current Liabilities (net working capital)}}$	A specific measure of the degree of vulnerability to a possible drop in the value of inventories.
Operating Efficiency	$\dfrac{\text{Cost of Goods Sold (does not include sales and administrative expenses)}}{\text{Net Sales}}$	Fixed charges may or may not be included. Measures the efficiency of production processes.
Productivity of Assets	$\dfrac{\text{Capacity in Units}}{\text{Fixed Investment}}$	A measure of the productivity of facilities and equipment.
Asset Utilization	$\dfrac{\text{Production in Units}}{\text{Capacity in Units}}$	A measure of the degree of capacity being utilized.
Asset Turnover (effectiveness or efficiency, as the case may be; effectiveness refers to the market results, efficiency refers to internal results)	$\dfrac{\text{Cost of Goods Sold}}{\text{Inventory}}$	Inventory turnover.
	$\dfrac{\text{Net Sales}}{\text{Total Assets}}$	A measure of total or fixed assets turnover. This can reflect excessive investment or overtrading of assets.

TABLE 2.6.   SELECTED RATIOS FOR ORGANIZATIONAL ANALYSIS
(CONTINUED)

THE STATE THAT IS MEASURED	THE RATIO	SOME EXPLANATORY COMMENTS
	$\dfrac{\text{Net Sales or Cost of Goods Sold}}{\text{Fixed Assets}}$	A measure of total or fixed assets turnover. This can reflect excessive investment or overtrading of assets.
Credit Management Efficiency	$\dfrac{\text{Accounts Receivables}}{\text{Average Daily Credit Sales}}$	A measure of the average collection period.
Adequacy of Working Capital	$\dfrac{\text{Working Capital}}{\text{Total Assets}}$	A measure of the allocation of resources between working capital and fixed assets.
Profitability	$\dfrac{\text{Profit before Taxes, Interest, and Extraordinary Items}}{\text{Total Assets (total investment)}}$	A measure of the profitability of the organization without respect to the vagaries of financial structure, certain nonrepeating costs and windfalls, or tax position. This allows for a more accurate comparison with a previous year or with organizations in a similar line of endeavor.
	$\dfrac{\text{Net Profit After Taxes}}{\text{Total Assets}}$	A measure of net return on investment (ROI).
	$\dfrac{\text{Net Profit After Taxes}}{\text{Net Sales}}$	A measure of net profit margin.

TABLE 2.6.   SELECTED RATIOS FOR ORGANIZATIONAL ANALYSIS
(CONTINUED)

THE STATE THAT IS MEASURED	THE RATIO	SOME EXPLANATORY COMMENTS
	$$\frac{\text{Profit before Taxes, Interest, and Extraordinary Items}}{\text{Net Sales}}$$	A measure of net operating margin.
Financial Leverage	$$\frac{\text{Total Liabilities}}{\text{Tangible Net Worth}} \quad \text{or} \quad \frac{\text{Fixed Liabilities}}{\text{Tangible Net Worth}}$$	Measure the degree to which risk has been transferred to creditors and the degree of caution to be exercised by creditors.
Operating Leverage	$$\frac{\text{Increase in Profit before Taxes, Interest, or Extraordinary Items (in percent)}}{\text{Increase in Units Sold (in percent)}}$$	Measures the effect of an increase in sales volume upon profits.
Profitability for Owners	$$\frac{\text{Net Profit After Taxes}}{\text{Equity}}$$	Measures the return on a historical equity value.
	$$\frac{\text{Dividends per Share}}{\text{Market Price per Share}}$$	A measure of the yield on the value placed upon the organization by the investment community.
	$$\frac{\text{Market Price per Share}}{\text{Earnings per Share}}$$	Known as the price-earnings ratio.

referenced. For example, profit, sales, cost, turnover, or morale are the type of result indices that can be used.

Although, theoretically, a broad array of ratios can be developed, care must be exercised so that the appropriate ratio is chosen for measuring the degree of state achievement. The point is that the user must understand just what a particular ratio actually measures and fully grasp its limitations.

With that note of caution, I have listed in Table 2.6 selected ratios that represent some of the more widely utilized measures for organizational analysis. What they purport to measure is also given. Rule-of-thumb values have from time to time been established for some of these ratios, but the ease with which some ratios can be manipulated (for example, the current ratio), as well as the diversity of situational and environmental situations, mitigate against a rigid use of such rules of thumb.

DATA SHEET FOR ACTIVITY-INTERACTION ANALYSIS

Column 1 of the Data Sheet for Activity-Interaction Analysis (Table 2.7) identifies the result index under consideration. Column 2 suggests the various activity-interaction categories that may be investigated. Column 3 identifies the various units of analysis in which inappropriate activities may occur; its subheadings provide space for noting discrepancies. Column 4 may be used to briefly record any apparent reasons for inappropriate behaviors. Here an effort should be made to identify any inappropriate management actions that appear to be related to the inappropriate behavior. The table also includes an example of data relating to the activity-interaction analysis.

DATA SHEET FOR AFTER-THE-FACT
RESOURCE CAPABILITIES ANALYSIS

The Data Sheet for After-the-Fact Resource Capabilities

Analysis (Table 2.8) may be used to record any apparent deficiencies in resources that existed during the period under review. The first column provides the result index; the second column, the resource category; the third column, the resource measure. (Some examples of resource categories and measures are provided in the Table 2.9.) The fourth asks for actual resource inadequacies that existed over the period in which significant deviations were found. The fifth column provides space for recording any short- and long-term premises with respect to resource capabilities that were made at the beginning of the year or fiscal period under review. Column six searches for reasons (preferably decisions of management) for resource deficiencies or, for that matter, for possible inappropriate or erroneous planning premises with respect to the expected capabilities. In the final column any interim changes that may have been made with respect to deficiencies or inappropriate planning premises should be recorded.

It may appear that resource capabilities are assessed twice, once at the results analysis stage and again at the resource capabilities analysis stage. Although some duplication may occur, actually two readings are taken with respect to resources to ensure that any possible deficiencies are not overlooked. In results analysis, the results of resource activities are analyzed for significant deviations from standards, while in results capabilities analysis, actual resource capabilities needed but unavailable during the review period are noted. In the first instance, for example, accounting or data processing may have set a target for accurate and on-time performance. Results analysis would evaluate performance against that target. In the second case, results capabilities analysis attempts to identify resource deficiencies actually experienced by an operations unit. For example, production may have lacked the "right kind" of cost data, and this deficiency would be picked up in results capabilities analysis.

TABLE 2.7. DATA SHEET FOR ACTIVITY-INTERACTION ANALYSIS

(1)	(2)	(3) Inappropriate Activity (by unit of analysis)									(4)
		Line Activity				Resource Activity				Organization Level	
Result Index	Activity-Interaction Category	Mfg.	Mrktg.	Logistics	R&D	Acquisition	Maintenance & Develop	Compensation	Retirement		Some Reasons for Inappropriate Activities-Interactions (decisions)
Cost (Example)	Work Flow	Irregular									Failure to schedule jobs
	Adherence to Policies-Rules										
	Behaviorial Pattern	Employees stockpile									
	Motivation—Effort Exerted										
	Communication Patterns										

112

Leadership Style									
Situational Characteristics									
Technology									
Power									
Expectations									
Supervision									
Other									

Example: In the above case, costs were above targets due to an irregular flow of jobs to work stations. This resulted in considerable slack time as well as rush periods for the workers. As a result, they would stockpile their output whenever possible in order to protect their daily output quota. The lack of sophisticated scheduling techniques was found to be responsible.

TABLE 2.8. DATA SHEET FOR AFTER-THE-FACT RESOURCE CAPABILITIES ANALYSIS

(1) Result Index	(2) Resource Category	(3) Resource Measure	(4) Actual Resource Inadequacies	(5) Planning Premises (for review period) Short Run	(5) Planning Premises (for review period) Long Run	(6) Some Reasons for Resource Deficiencies or for Inappropriate Planning Premises with Respect to Expected Capabilities (over review period)	(7) Interim Changes Made with Respect to Deficiencies or Inappropriate Planning Premises, if Any (during review period)
Example: Cost	Semiskilled employees	Experience	Most employees in this group had less than one year's experience in this unit	Anticipated a 50-50 mix of workers with less than one year's longevity	None	Did not anticipate the 3-month layoff that resulted in a permanent loss of most of the experienced workers (Note: The cause for this situation requires further investigation)	None

114

The table also provides an example of the type of information that would be recorded for a resource-capabilities analysis.

TABLE 2.9.   SOME POSSIBLE CATEGORIES AND SOME
MEASURES OF RESOURCE CAPABILITIES

RESOURCE CATEGORY	RESOURCE MEASURES
Human Resources	
Management	Age
Professionals	Experience
Technicians	Sex
Semiskilled	Number
Physical and Natural Resources	
Plant	Age
Equipment	Capacity
Raw Materials	Cost
Location	Size
Information Resources	
Forecasts	Accuracy
Market demand	Timeliness
Supply market	
Competitors' activities	
Financial Resources	
Working capital	Amount
Line of credit	Cost
Leverage capabilities	
Technological Capabilities	
(with respect to each business function)	Age
	Cost
Product-Service Capabilities	
Product	Size
Service	Image
Dealers	Quality
Channel of distribution	Exclusiveness
	Uniqueness

DATA SHEET FOR AN AFTER-THE-FACT
ENVIRONMENTAL PROFILE

The Data Sheet for an After-the-Fact Environmental Profile (Table 2.10) provides a framework for reconstruction of
the significant and relevant environmental forces as they actually existed during the period under review. The initial column provides the result index reference. The next two columns
provide space for designating the environmental categories of
relevance to the analysis and the measures or characteristics
used to describe the relevant forces. (Some examples of these
categories and measures are listed in Table 2.11.) The fourth
column asks for actual conditions that prevailed during the
review period; and the fifth column, the planning premises
for the short and the long run that were used for decision
making. The sixth column is used to record some reasons for
discrepancies between premises and actual environmental conditions. The seventh column is used to record any interim
arrangements that may have been made with respect to any
unexpected environmental conditions. The last column is used
to identify specific decisions that could conceivably have been
inappropriate in light of the environmental conditions as they
actually existed during the period under review. An example is
shown on the sample data sheet.

The environmental analysis focuses attention on a number
of important areas. First, it calls for a review of all relevant
and significant environmental forces that might provide some
direction in discovering causes for significant deviations.
Second, it inquires into the planning premises, suggesting that
assumptions are necessary for effective planning and that these
should have been made explicit. Third, it asks for some possible reasons for discrepancies between planning premises and
actual market conditions, thus, in effect, initiating a preliminary review of market research, forecasting, and, perhaps, the
management information system. Fourth, it asks that any interim decisions, which represented responses to the unexpected

TABLE 2.10.   DATA SHEET FOR AN AFTER-THE-FACT ENVIRONMENTAL PROFILE

(1)	(2)	(3)	(4)	(5) Planning Premises (for review period)		(6)	(7)	(8)
				Short Run	Long Run			
Result Index	Environmental Category	Measure or Characteristic	Actual Conditions Existing during Review Period			Some Reasons for Discrepancies between Premises and Actual Conditions	What Interim Changes Were Made with Respect to Actual Environmental Conditions?	What Specific Decisions Appear Inappropriate in View of Actual Environmental Conditions?
Example:								
Cost	Nature of the supply market	Number of vendors	Supplier moved away	None made	None made		Attempted to produce own parts	Purchasing policy favoring single suppliers

market circumstances, be made explicit, thus suggesting an interim review of their effectiveness. Finally, it asks that those decisions that conceivably could have been affected by the unexpected market conditions be identified so that they can be reevaluated.

TABLE 2.11.   SOME EXAMPLES OF ENVIRONMENTAL
                        CATEGORIES AND MEASURES

ENVIRONMENTAL CATEGORY	MEASURE OR CHARACTERISTIC
Nature of the Industry	Capacity
	Value added
	Specialized, integrated, diversified
	Growing, static, declining
	Capital, technology, or labor intensive
	Fixed costs to total costs — relationships
	Distribution channels used
Nature of the Product or Service	Availability of substitutes
	Type — industrial, consumer, service
	Susceptibility to economic fluctuations
	Production characteristics
	Stage in product life cycle
	Cost-price relationship
Nature of the Buyers	Credit needs
	Number
	Size
	Preferences
	Buying habits
	Types of buyers
Nature of the Competition	Number
	Size
	Dominant competitive tool
	Pricing strategies
	Product-market strategies

TABLE 2.11. SOME EXAMPLES OF ENVIRONMENTAL CATEGORIES AND MEASURES (CONTINUED)

ENVIRONMENTAL CATEGORY	MEASURE OR CHARACTERISTIC
Nature of the Supply Market	Number of sources of supply
	Size of vendors
	Availability of substitutes
	Location
	Pricing policy
Economic Conditions	Inflation, deflation, stability
	Interest rates
	Growth, stability, stagnation
Government Aids or Regulations	Product
	Pricing
	Manufacturing
	Taxes
	Financial
	Employee relations
	Wages, hours, working conditions
	Economic, monetary, and fiscal policies
	Consolidations, mergers
Social Climate	Consumerism
	Ethical values
	Demographic characteristics
	Attitudes toward work, authority
Union Climate	Passive-militant
	Bargaining unit
	Union-management relations
	Type of demands
Political Climate	Liberal — conservative
	Democratic — autocratic
	Stable — unstable

Strategic decisions, particularly, represent an organization's special response to its environment, on the one hand, and to its resource capabilities, on the other hand. The nature of such decisions, of course, is influenced by the decision makers' perceptions of the environment and of the organization resources. The appropriateness of such decisions, therefore, may be found by observing actual environment conditions and actual resource capabilities during the period that is under review. Implementing or tactical decisions, although in part an outgrowth of strategic decisions, may also be conditioned by the environment and the resource variables.

DECISION AND INFLUENCE CHECKLIST

The Decision and Influence Checklist (Table 2.12) represents a summary of the kinds of decisions that were discussed earlier and their constituent parts. It is intended to aid the problem finder by suggesting decision areas that might be directly or indirectly contributing to significant deviations. The types of decisions are listed on the left side and the corresponding units of analysis are provided as column headings. Spaces provided by this matrix can be used as a checkoff chart or to note areas that may need investigation.

AFTER-THE-FACT RESUMÉ SHEET

The After-the-Fact Resumé Sheet (Table 2.13) summarizes the decisions that the problem finder has associated with the significant deviations. Column 1 lists the result indices, and the ensuing columns detail the decisions relating thereto.

The inappropriate decisions are drawn from the data sheets for activity-interaction analysis (column 2), resource capabilities analysis (column 3), and the environment profile (columns 4 and 5). An example is shown in the table. The data are taken from the examples provided in the supporting data sheets. In this example, the problem finder had identified an increase in the unit cost of production with poor scheduling, a purchasing policy that proved to be shortsighted, and a layoff policy that had unexpected consequences. All three decisions require careful review in order to counteract the rise in unit production costs.

TABLE 2.12. DECISION AND INFLUENCE CHECKLIST

Decisions	Components	Customer	Owner	Employee	Supplier	Community	Comments
Objectives	Needs and Markets						
	States						
	Priorities of States						
	Creed						
External Strategy	Product/Service/Output						
	Specific Recipients						
	Line Functions						
	Manufacturing						
	Marketing						
	Logistics						
	R and D						

Decisions	Components	Physical Assets	Human	Financial	Technol.	Information
		Orgl. Level	Mfg. Group	Mktg. Group	R&D Group	Other Units	Comments
Internal Strategy	Resource Functions					
	Acquisition					
	Compensation					
	Maint. & Develop.					
	Retirement					
	Factors					
	State of Environment					

continued

121

TABLE 2.12. DECISION AND INFLUENCE CHECKLIST (CONTINUED)

Decisions	Components	Orgl. Level	Mfg. Group	Mktg. Group	R&D Group	Other Units	Comments
Work Evaluation	Results						
	Target Range						
	Signif. Deviations						
	Appropriate Target						
Work Procedures or Methods							
Work Schedules							
Work Sequences							
Work Loads							
Extra-organizational Influences	Goals						
	Needs						
	Attitudes						
(Individual or Group)	Values						
	Beliefs						

	State & Group Priorities
	Product-Market Characteristics
	Technological Charisteristics
	Personal Factors
Organization Structure	Division of work
	Functional
	Divisional
	Venture
	Special (hybrid)
	Method of Integration
	Authority
	Competence
	Grass Roots
Resource Allocation	Resource Specification
	Support Level
Work Assignment	Formal Job Conditions Desired
	Human States Desired
Authority Delegation	Formal Job Conditions Desired
	Human States Desired
	States
Work Standards	Yardstick
	Resource Capabilities
	Situational Circumstances
	Target Range

TABLE 2.13. AFTER-THE-FACT RESUMÉ SHEET

(1) Significant Deviation Result Indices	(2) Activity-Interaction Analysis Contributing Decisions	(3) Resource Capabilities Analysis Contributing Decisions	(4) Environment Profile Conditions	(5) Possible Inappropriate Decisions
Example: Cost	Scheduling	Layoff Policy	Supplier Moved	Purchasing Policy

Review of the Model for Problem Finding, After the Fact

The model for problem finding, after the fact, shown in Fig. 2.10, illustrates the basic approach to after-the-fact problem finding. Beginning at the top left, (1) significant deviations are found; (2) inappropriate activity-interaction behaviors are identified for each significant deviation, and possible reasons are suggested; (3) deficiencies in resource capabilities for the review period for each significant deviation are found, and reasons are suggested; and (4) the actual and premised environment is recalled with reference to each significant deviation, and possible inappropriate decisions are identified in view of unexpected developments. The four sources of possible inappropriate decisions are then sorted into hierarchical chains to facilitate problem solving.

Developing the Hierarchy of Causes (Decisions)

After causes have been identified, a hierarchy may on occasion be constructed in order to direct the problem finder's focus upon the most basic causes. For example, when a selling procedure as well as the choice of market are found inappropriate, a new market strategy must first be formulated before the selling procedure is considered. Perhaps a revised market choice will, in effect, dictate the selling procedure. Selling to an industrial market, for example, will usually require different selling tactics than selling to a retail market. Some decisions may not be related, and these can then be considered as separate subjects for problem solving.

ARE ALL SIGNIFICANT DEVIATIONS EXPLAINED? THE CHECK

Before problem solving can commence, a check must be made to ensure that the causes that have been identified in fact adequately explain all significant deviations. When the problem finder is reasonably satisfied, problem solving can begin, starting with the most basic cause of a series of inter-

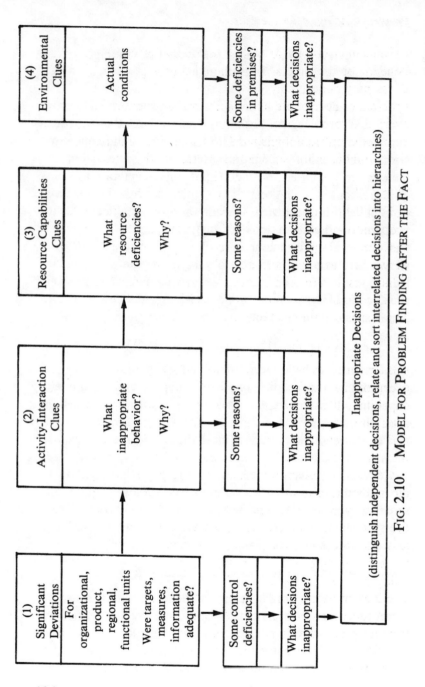

FIG. 2.10. MODEL FOR PROBLEM FINDING AFTER THE FACT

(distinguish independent decisions, relate and sort interrelated decisions into hierarchies)

dependent decisions or with a cause that is considered independent of the others. For example, new purchasing procedures may conceivably be considered without reference to a problem of developing a new motivation program. Note, however, that problem solving at the operations level is never completed unless a management system analysis has been conducted. That is the subject of chapter 3.

AN EXAMPLE OF PROBLEM FINDING, AFTER THE FACT

Fig. 2.11 illustrates the contributions of each step of the problem-finding process.

Column 1 shows a hierarchy of results. A drop in ROI is shown here as arising from a drop in sales revenue. Two subsidiary results are used to explain the sales income drop—i.e., the decrease in gross profit margin and excessive sales returns. The last two results become the focus for the problem finder, since they explain the other significant deviations.

Column 2, Activity-Interaction Clues, notes that excessive sales returns were caused by the tendency of salesmen to overpromote the product in terms of product performance capability. This tendency, in turn, resulted from a lack of sales supervision.

The decrease in gross profit margin is shown as resulting from a price cut.

Column 3 provides some interesting resource capabilities clues. First, the company's product was competitively inferior, so price was cut. Second, a shortage of sales supervisors brought about a lack of supervision. The shortage, in turn, was due to opening several new branches. This implemented the company's product-market strategy of intensively developing its present market area with its current product line. The lack of supervisors reflects a breakdown in implementing the product-market strategy since a provision for a supervisory training program was not made.

Column 4, Environmental Clues, notes that the inferiority of the product was due to the competitor introducing a new

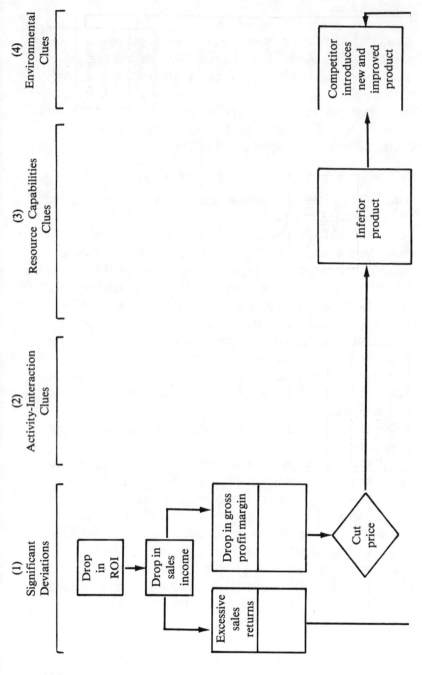

| (1)
Significant
Deviations | (2)
Activity-Interaction
Clues | (3)
Resource Capabilities
Clues | (4)
Environmental
Clues |

128

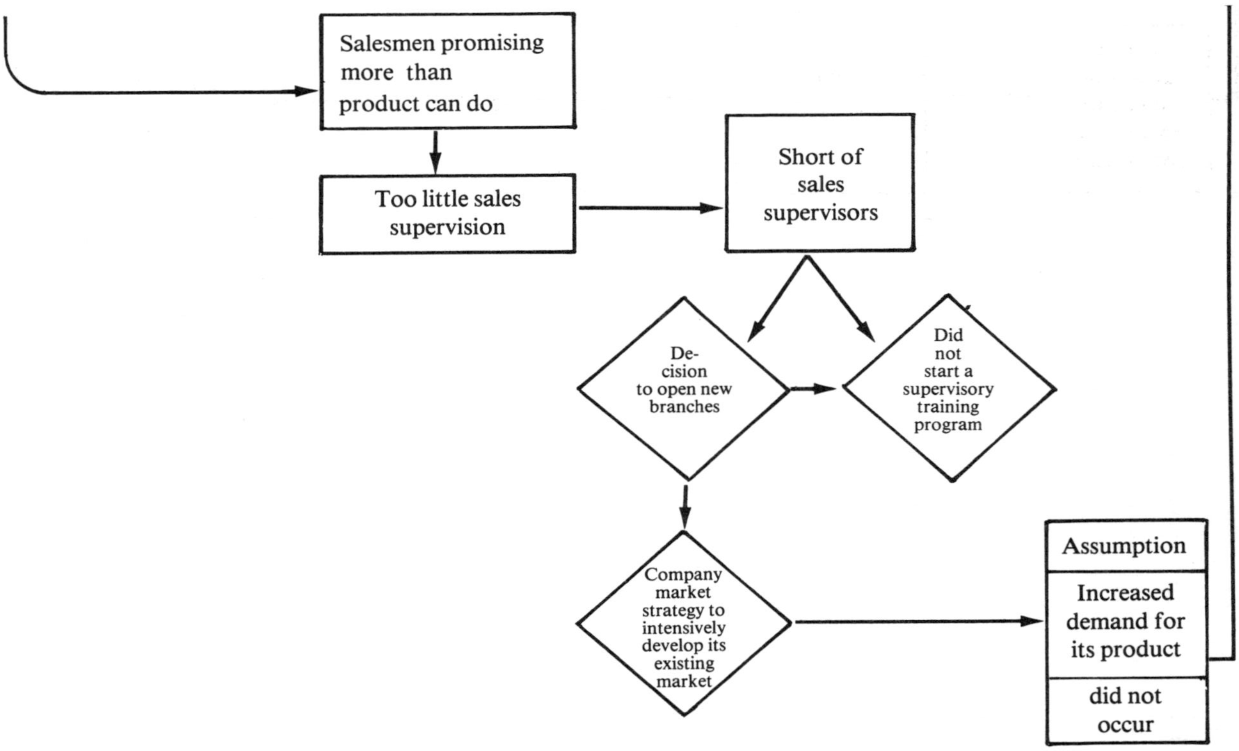

Fig. 2.11. AN EXAMPLE OF PROBLEM FINDING, AFTER THE FACT

The diagram shows the following flow:

- Salesmen promising more than product can do → Too little sales supervision → Short of sales supervisors
- Short of sales supervisors → Did not start a supervisory training program
- Short of sales supervisors → Decision to open new branches
- Decision to open new branches → Did not start a supervisory training program
- Decision to open new branches → Company market strategy to intensively develop its existing market
- Company market strategy to intensively develop its existing market → Assumption: Increased demand for its product did not occur
- Assumption box connects back to Salesmen promising more than product can do

129

and improved product line. The product-market strategy is pinpointed as one of the fundamental inappropriate decisions as it was based on an erroneous assumption of increased demand. The assumption failed to materialize due to the introduction of the competitive product.

The flow chart's symbols that fall toward the right and toward the bottom will usually reflect the most basic variables that require attention. In this case, erroneous planning assumptions led to an inappropriate product-market strategy. Inappropriate implementation is evident in terms of the lack of a supervisor development program. The competitor's product reflects a critical environmental change with which the organization must contend.

Among the causes, the breakdown in market surveillance is perhaps most basic; product-market strategy would be second; the lack of supervisory training, third. However, in order of immediate need, product-market strategy should probably be reviewed first. Pending a decision here, the training problem could be tabled, since the nature of the training needed might depend upon the direction the revised product-market strategy took.

Not indicated in the flow chart are two problems that need further analysis. First, Why the breakdown in market surveillance? and second, Why the failure to fully implement the new branch program?

THE RELATIONSHIP BETWEEN OPERATIONS ANALYSIS AND MANAGEMENT ANALYSIS

After completing the problem-finding analysis, many organizations probably feel satisfied that their poor performance record is well on the way to being corrected. After all, if schedules are inappropriate, then all that must be done is to determine more appropriate schedules. Or, if the product-market strategy is inappropriate for today's market situation, a change that conforms more closely to the situational demands should solve the problem. However, a very critical element is thus overlooked. The management or governance system that produced the inappropriate decision or that failed to update its approach to market conditions is left untouched. And there is a reasonably high probability that similar deficiencies will recur in the future if the defect in the management system is not discovered and corrected. While operations analysis seeks to unearth causes for poor performance in terms of decisions or, possibly, environmental circumstances, management analysis seeks to discover deficiencies in the system that produced inappropriate responses. This is the subject of chapter 3. That kind of analysis is too often overlooked. It strikes at the very heart of organizational life. Not only does it deal directly with the capabilities of managers and executives, but it also could involve their personal goals and ambitions—should these personal factors appear to be playing an inordinate role in the decision-making process of those managers.

References and Suggested Readings

REFERENCES

Ansoff, H. J., and Brandenburg, R. G. "A Language for Organization Design: Parts I and II." *Management Science,* August, 1971, pp. B-705–31. (Provides a detailed analysis of the basic types of structure and their many variations.)

Argyris, Chris. *Integrating the Individual and the Organization.* New York: John Wiley & Sons, 1964.

Dalton, Gene W., Lawrence, Paul R., and Lorsch, Jay W. *Organizational Structure and Design.* Homewood, Ill.: Richard D. Irwin and The Dorsey Press, 1970. Pp. 1–16.

Dearden, John. "Appraising Profit Center Manager." *Harvard Business Review,* May-June, 1968, pp. 80–87.

Dearden, John. "The Case against ROI Control." *Harvard Business Review,* May-June, 1968, pp. 124–35.

Donnelly, John F., an interview with. "Participative Management at Work." *Harvard Business Review,* Jan.-Feb., 1977, pp. 117–27.

Dunnette, M.D., Campbell, J. P., and Hakel, M. D. "Factors Contributing to Job Satisfaction and Job Dissatisfaction in Six Occupational Groups." *Organizational Behavior and Human Performance* 2, no. 2 (1967), pp. 143–74.

Fiedler, Fred E. *A Theory of Leadership Effectiveness.* New York: McGraw-Hill, 1967. (The material on leadership styles and situational factors has been adapted in part from Fred E. Fiedler.)

Henderson, Bruce D., and Dearden, John. "New System for Divisional Control." *Harvard Business Review,* Sept.-Oct., 1966, pp. 144–60.

Henrici, Stanley B. "Eyeing the ROI." *Harvard Business Review,* May-June, 1968, pp. 88–97.

Herzberg, Frederick. *Work and the Nature of Man.* World Publishing Co., 1966.

Holden, Paul E., Pederson, Carlton A., and Germane, Gayton E. *Top Management.* New York: McGraw-Hill, 1968. Pp. 25–27.

Lee, James A. "Behavioral Theory vs. Reality." *Harvard Business Review,* March-April, 1971, pp. 20 ff.

Likert, Renis. *New Patterns of Management.* New York: McGraw-Hill, 1961.

Lorsch, Jay W., and Lawrence, Paul R. "Organizing for Product Innovation." *Harvard Business Review,* Jan.-Feb., 1965. Reprinted in *Organizational Structure and Design,* edited by Gene W. Dalton, Paul R. Lawrence, and Jay W. Lorsch. Homewood, Ill.: Richard D. Irwin and The Dorsey Press, 1970. Pp. 280–96.

Maslow, Abraham H. *Motivation and Personality.* New York: Harper & Row, 1954.

McGregor, Caroline, and Bennis, W. G., eds. *The Professional Manager.* New York: McGraw-Hill, 1967.

McGregor, Douglas. *The Human Side of Enterprise.* New York: McGraw-Hill, 1960.

Odiorne, George S. *Management by Objectives.* New York: Pitman Publishing Corp., 1965. Pp. 54–67.

Price, James L. *Organizational Effectiveness: An Inventory of Propositions.* Homewood, Ill.: Richard D. Irwin, 1968. Pp. 11–12.

Reddin, W. J. *Managerial Effectiveness.* New York: McGraw-Hill, 1970. (The material on leadership styles and situational factors has been adapted in part from W. J. Reddin.)

Schiff, J. S., and Schiff, Michael. "New Management Tool: ROAM." *Harvard Business Review,* July-August, 1967, pp. 59–66.

Schleh, Edward C. *Management by Results.* New York: McGraw-Hill, n.d. Pp. 40, 216.

Van de Ven, Andrew H. *Group Decision Making and Effectiveness—An Experimental Study.* Kent, Ohio: Kent State University Press, 1974.

Van de Ven, Andrew H., and Delbecq, Andre L. "Nominal versus Interacting Groups for Committee Decision Making Effectiveness." *Academy of Management Journal,* June, 1971, pp. 203–12.

Vroom, Victor H., and Deci, Edward L., eds. *Management and Motivation.* Victoria, Australia: Penguin Books, 1973.

Walker, Arthur H., and Lorsch, Jay W. "Organizational Choice: Product vs. Function." *Harvard Business Review,* November-December, 1968, pp. 129–38.

Whyte, William Foote. *Organizational Behavior Theory and Application.* Homewood, Ill.: Richard D. Irwin and The Dorsey Press, 1969. Pp. 100–101.

SUGGESTED READINGS

Cammann, Cortlandt, and Nadler, David A. "Fit Control Systems to Your Managerial Style." *Harvard Business Review,* Jan.-Feb., 1976, pp. 65–72.

Committe, T. C. *Managerial Finance for the Seventies.* New York: McGraw-Hill, 1972.

Dean, Joel. "Pricing Policies for New Products." *Harvard Business Review,* Nov.-Dec., 1976, pp. 141–53.

Holloman, Charles R., and Hendrick, Hal W. "Adequacy of Group Decisions as a Function of the Decision-Making Process." *Academy of Management Journal,* June, 1972, pp. 175–84.

Juran, J. M. *Managerial Breakthrough: A Systematic Approach to Improving Management Performance.* New York: McGraw-Hill, 1965.

Katz, Robert L. "Skills of an Effective Administrator." *Harvard Business Review,* Sept.-Oct. 1974, pp. 90–102.

Kepner, Charles H., and Tregoe, Benjamin B. *The Rational Manager.* New York: McGraw-Hill, 1965.

Key Business Ratios in 125 Lines, 1973. New York: Dun & Bradstreet, 1974. (Published annually.)

Koontz, Harold. *Appraising Managers as Managers.* New York: McGraw-Hill, 1971.

Leavitt, Harold J., Dell, William R., and Eyring Henry B. *The Organizational World.* New York: Harcourt Brace Jovanovich, 1973.

McKinsey & Co. Staff Members. *The Art of Top Management: A McKinsey Anthology.* New York: McGraw-Hill Book Co., 1970.

Redden, W. J. *Effective Management by Objectives.* New York: McGraw-Hill Book Co., 1971.

Shepherd, Clovis R. *Small Groups—Some Sociological Perspectives.* San Francisco: Chandler Publishing Co., 1964. (An excellent summary of small group attributes and processes.)

Sherwin, Douglas S. "Management of Objectives." *Harvard Business Review,* May-June, 1976, pp. 149–60.

3

Problem Finding, After the Fact—Management System Analysis

Introduction

An analysis of operating systems should usually lead to an identification of inappropriate decisions when significant deviations are present. On the other hand, an analysis of the management systems that produced the inappropriate decisions represents an attempt to uncover deficiencies in the management decision-making system itself so that recurrence of similar inappropriate decisions will be minimized.

The management system can be visualized by means of the model shown in Table 3.1.

TABLE 3.1.   A MODEL OF THE MANAGEMENT SYSTEM

Decisions and Influences	Resource Capabilities	Activity-Interaction	Output
Imposed administrative constraints Self-imposed decisions Extraorganizational influences	Decision-makers Information Time	Decision making	Decisions

The model illustrates three areas of interest—activity-interaction, resource capabilities, and decisions and influences. The first of these, activity-interaction, is, in fact, the decision-making process. Resource capabilities represent, by and large, information, time, and the decision makers themselves. Decisions and influences are the governors of the system and thus represent the decisions imposed by the hierarchy upon a given management system. They include decisions that are self-imposed, such as some past decision that might serve as a precedent; self-imposed procedures for ordering the decision-making process; or extraorganizational influences that might affect the nature of the resultant decision.

Decision-Making Process

Working back through the system, the activity-interaction cell—i.e., the decision-making process—is the first area for observation or, if possible, recall. Relatively little is actually known about just how organizations make decisions. Many studies describe the process as it has been gleaned from questionnaires or interview data. Occasionally, some real insights are obtained, but the validity of such methods is generally rather uninspiring. This is still the "black box" of the management system. While some generalities can be deduced from studies about how the decision-making process is actually conducted, many normative statements are readily available regarding how the process *should* be carried on.

The reason for the reluctance of managers to "open up" the process is obvious. First, the decisions themselves are often competitive weapons that are intended for the eyes and ears of corporate personnel only. Second, there is probably considerable natural reluctance to expose personal deficiencies to those who want to study the process. Third, personal aspirations are hard to justify on corporate grounds. Personal motives must remain submerged, and a trained observer might just suspect their presence and their attendant influence.[1]

A great deal has been written about T-groups and sensitivity training as means for managers to understand their personal mode of operating and their personal impact upon others (Schein and Bennis; Howard). However, there does not appear to be a consensus as to the effectiveness of T-group training (Paine; Drotning). The reports of such exercises have demonstrated, however, the crucial impact that behavorial mechanisms and personal needs and goals may have upon the decision-making process.

An evaluation of the decision-making process can, under the circumstances, probably best be carried on by the "insider" as a formal member of that process. In so doing, it should be recognized that the process essentially involves interactions with people and with information. Therefore, the attitudes one expresses toward information and toward people

---

1. At a leadership seminar conducted on the West Coast some years ago the speaker related to participants his personal experience with a multi-university faculty committee. Several days had been allotted for preparing a special seminar program. Over half the allotted time was devoted to getting the "hidden agenda" out of the way before any real progress could be discerned with respect to the actual purpose of the meeting. In essence, the substantive business was probably attended to only after everyone had been given the opportunity to convince his peers how well qualified he was to be a participating member of that committee.

vitally affect the whole decision-making process. Some suggested areas that could be investigated include the following:

- Were the decision makers overwhelmed with too much data input and with too little rationale for sorting it all out? The data relevant to the problem must be retained, the irrelevant ignored. The significant data must be sorted from the insignificant.
- Were administrative constraints considered? For example, did established priorities play an appropriate role in the decision-making process? Were the constraints observed?
- Were environmental opportunities, threats, constraints, and obstacles logically and unemotionally considered?
- Were current resource capabilities adequately assessed with respect to expected resource requirements over the planning period?
- Was the leadership style that was used in the decision-making process appropriate to the situational demands? (See action-interaction analysis, leadership styles, chapter 2.)
- Was the means for deciding upon a course of action appropriate to the situation—by vote, consensus, or unilateral action?
- Was corporate philosophy considered—i.e., corporate attitude toward risk, time, work, or people?
- Was a systematic process used in weighing the costs and benefits of each alternative?
- Were decision makers taking premature positions prior to the introduction of all of the relevant data?
- Did the process reflect undue defensiveness on the part of participants? (See action-interaction analysis, behavioral patterns, chapter 2.)

Deficiencies in the decision-making process may be a direct reflection upon one or more of the participants. Deficiencies will often provide clues that will route the problem finder directly back to the resources used or available for use in the decision-making process. Decision-making process deficiencies may also have occurred as a result of administrative constraints or extraorganizational influences under which the system operated.

The Adequacy of Resources

Decision making rests on several prime resources—the data to be evaluated, the evaluators, and the time available for making the decision.

The Data as a Resource

The decision is usually only as effective as the information on which it is based. The lead time required to assemble a reasonably complete data package may at times run into years of effort. Full information is an elusive and unrealistic aim. At some point a cutoff must be made. Knowing what information to acquire is no little task in itself (Zani).

An evaluation of the data bank that was utilized for a decision can be made on some of the following dimensions:

RAW INFORMATION

- Is it reasonably sufficient—i.e., does it represent a fair coverage of relevant and significant factors?
- Is it current? Has it been updated?
- Is the information accurate and based on the best sources available (Aguilon; Ference)? If not, is the source made explicit? Are approximations labeled as such? The data validity, among other considerations, may be a function of context—i.e., the context in which the information was developed and the context in which it is to be applied. The question that must be asked then is, Does the application match the original frame of reference? (McDonough).

COMPARATIVE INFORMATION

- Are appropriate factors used against which raw data are compared? For example, the choice of a particular base period could affect the attractiveness of a ratio.

- Are percentages backed up by original figures? For example, a 50-percent increase may be misleading unless absolute figures are also provided.

Kinds of Data Involved in Decision Making

Decision makers should possess data related to all relevant and significant aspects of a contemplated course of action. Some suggested kinds of data follow.

- Alternative courses of action for evaluation
- Environmental opportunities, constraints, threats, obstacles—current and those expected during the planning horizon
- Administrative constraints imposed by the hierarchy
- Resource requirements for each alternative
- Resource capabilities—current and expected during the planning horizon
- The critical success activity—i.e., what must be done exceedingly well in order for the course of action to be successful? This may be a management activity or a line of resource-related activity
- Costs and benefits associated with each alternative: qualitative and quantitative; expected results with respect to all relevant interest groups; anticipated effects with respect to the activity itself; the expected consequences of the output; and the expected effects upon organizational resources
- The cutoff points for eliminating alternatives from further contention

Usually, some data will take the form of forecasts. However, a simple extension of trends can be misleading. Experts and specialists can seldom reach full agreement. The more sophisticated econometric models and regression equations are at times unreliable and often provocative; they are perhaps necessary but not sufficient in themselves. Some executives report that they put very little weight on the data provided by these forecasts. Their justifications are that un-

suspected variables may suddenly negate the model's forecasts, and qualitative features cannot effectively be built into
the model (Vancil; Dory and Lord; Glueck). Forecasts should
explicitly state the premises or assumptions upon which they
are based so that a future evaluation is feasible.

Sources of Data

The manager may assign the task of data collection to staff
individuals. In certain complex situations, it may be advisable
to provide the opportunity for all who will be affected by a
decision to be heard. In some large organizations, a planning
group may call for, collect, assemble, and evaluate input data
and then recommend a course of action. The authority to
recommend may carry considerable weight, but then the dilemma of line and staff begins to develop. Although the data
bank may well be a neutral entity, it is difficult to divorce the
data from those who produced the information and, in the
case of staff advice, from those who make recommendations
concerning the data. This observation leads to the second
prime resource of the decision-making process, the decision
makers who are on the receiving end of the data and recommendations and must ultimately make the final decision.

Decision Makers as a Resource in the Decision-Making Process

The capability of decision makers becomes the central
theme when assessing the people who were involved in the
decision-making process. Some pertinent areas for inquiry
could include the following:

- Was the decision within the range of the decision makers'
  competences?
- Were those who would be directly affected by the decision consulted or asked to contribute? Were they a
  part of the resources utilized in the process?
- Did the decision makers reflect a healthy attitude toward
  their environment? A closed style tends to focus decision

makers upon their own department, and so they tend to
see all else as revolving around their own function or
product. Suboptimization and stagnation could develop.

- Did the decision makers reflect a healthy attitude toward
change?[2] In some instances, change evokes a self-
defeating reaction sequence involving denial, defensiveness, depression, then resignation (Glueck). Cooper
reports that major product innovations, for example, tend
to originate outside the current group (Cooper).

- Did the decision makers reflect an appropriate attitude
toward strategic, long-term planning deliberations?
Studies of management preferences show that many managers prefer the short-run, the more immediate problems,
rather than the long-term strategic problem situation
(Mintzberg).

- Did the decision makers reflect conflicting values in their
economic, social, political, or aesthetic preferences?
Deep-seated value conflicts often do exist; a divided
house may result, sapping energies in unproductive work.
Such conflicts may be resolved, or a reasonable com-
promise attained by identifying the areas of conflict as
well as the expected consequences of a contemplated
course of action. Often consequences can be found that
serve a wide range of values (Guth and Tagiuri).

- Did the decision makers reflect conflicting attitudes
toward risk, time, or people? Were they at considerable
variance with the organizational position? Differences
are inevitable and often valuable, but serious, deep-
seated divisions may result in a "least-common-denom-
inator" type of decision.

- Did the decision makers reflect a respectful attitude
toward specialists and professionals outside their area of
expertise? Research suggests that an essential ingredient

---

2. It is not to be inferred that a healthy attitude toward change always
involves embracing the change. Issues of morality, values, or principles may
require stern resistance.

for resolving intergroup conflict is respect for the expertise of each specialized area of endeavor (Lawrence and Seiler).

● Did the decision makers reflect a respectful attitude toward authority? A negative attitude may lead to decisions that circumvent the constraints established by higher management.

● Was the age of decision makers appropriate to the complexity of the decision? Taylor reports that older executives tend to devote a longer period of time to arriving at a decision. They also seek out more information, evaluate it more accurately, are less confident about their decision, but are more flexible in changing their position if new data suggest such a move (Taylor). This appears to suggest that a more complex situation should be resolved by more experienced executives.

Time as a Resource in the Decision-Making Process

Often overlooked in the assessment of resources is the amount of time available to the decision makers. When time is of the essence, having certain desirable information, consultations, and deliberations in depth may become impossible.

Administrative Constraints
and Extraorganizational Influences

Decisions can be channeled or modified by the guidelines, rules, or constraints imposed by the hierarchy upon a given decision-making group. This group, in turn, inevitably reduces its own flexibility through decisions that may serve as precedents for subsequent decisions. Decision-making groups also may set their own rules and regulations to guide their decision-making processes. Personal goals, ambitions, or aspirations may modify the direction a decision would have taken in the absence of such influences. In short, imposed decisions, prior or self-imposed decisions, and personal extraorganizational influences are avenues the problem finder should explore in order to uncover possible underlying causes for inappropriate decisions.

Imposed Decisions

The overall aim in analyzing the governance system is to isolate possible reasons for inappropriate decisions. While decision-making analysis and resource analysis may uncover important clues, the cause of such deficiencies is often traceable to administrative constraint imposed upon the system by a higher-level management system. For example, one company found itself losing market share and detected that one of its product groups could no longer effectively compete in the rapidly changing market. It found that the product line was not being updated because of the structural arrangements that kept the production group in the immediate operational seat of power. The production executives were evaluated on the basis of unit cost and therefore had little motivation to spend dollars for product improvement. In this case, the imposed constraint upon operating executives—unit cost—and the structural arrangements that provided the production group with the authority to direct the product group represented serious decision deficiencies. The origin of these inappropriate decisions was top management. Imposed decisions usually concern such matters as corporate objectives, organization structure, certain resource allocations, delegations of authority, work assignments, and work standards. These become the constraints within which a group must work.

Self-Imposed Decisions

A marketing group may be used to illustrate self-imposed decisions. Marketing may, for example, decide to emphasize advertising and to distribute products through manufacturer's agents. These decisions represent basic strategies that become the constraints within which implementing decisions must fall.

Personal Extraorganizational Influences

Personal extraorganizational influences may be demonstrated in a decision to use manufacturer's agents rather than salesmen when the choice stems from some personal insecurity on the part of a marketing head who feels threatened by ambitious salesmen. Other sources of extraorganizational influences could include pressures applied by small, informal work groups, peer groups, or hierarchical political alliances, or perhaps obligations owed to others within the organization. The common dimension of all such influences is that the motivation stems from either the personal interests of the decision maker or from self-seeking interests of those who apply pressure upon the decision maker. It is the way in which such self-interests are satisfied that often tends to run counter to organizational interests.

Check Out Higher Management Systems

As an ultimate exploratory adventure, the problem finder may want to determine why offending administrative constraints were imposed upon a given organizational unit. When a functional decision-making group is analyzed, the investigation may lead to the top-management decision-making system. When this is the case, the management system analysis must be repeated in order to determine what deficiencies actually existed in this system.

Summary

The analysis of management systems has one central object —to determine the causes for inappropriate decisions. The approach suggests that three areas should be checked—the decision-making process itself, the adequacy of resources, and the constraints and influences impinging upon the management system. Identifying the cause and finding a viable option to correct the deficiency are usually more elusive in management system analysis than in operations analysis. The reason for this is that the human element is a more prominent feature in the analysis of decision-making systems than in the analysis of operating systems. In addition, the problem finders may be forced to incriminate themselves in a management system analysis—an alternative they may not wish to contemplate.

Checklist for Management System Analysis

A checklist (Table 3.2) is provided to assist the problem finder in analyzing the three areas of the managerial system. It is intended to alert the problem finder to some of the most probable causes for inappropriate decisions. Space is available for adding other factors. Two columns are also provided, titled "OK" and "Check [this] Out." Financial support level has been added for the sake of completeness.

References and Suggested Readings

REFERENCES

Aguilon, Francis. *Scanning the Business Environment.* New York: Macmillan, 1967. (Some interesting questions are raised here regarding the primary source of data for larger organizations. The author reports that, the larger the organization, the greater the reliance on inside sources for data; that outside data are usually unsolicited despite the admission that they have greater relative impact. He also reports that verbal means are of greater importance than written; that the higher the level of the decision maker, the greater the reliance on verbal data; and that the written sources, in order of importance, comprise newspapers, trade journals, and company reports. This suggests a tendency for receiving filtered data from inside sources. In contrast, the small organizations without the capability for producing large amounts of inside data must place greater emphasis on outside sources. Thus one could tentatively conclude that with growth comes the tendency to close out more and more outside data.)

TABLE 3.2.   CHECKLIST FOR ANALYZING
MANAGEMENT DECISION-MAKING
SYSTEM

Management System: _____

Inappropriate Decision: _____

		DECISION-MAKING PROCESS
OK	Check Out	
		Sorting the Relevant from the Irrelevant
		Sorting the Significant from the Insignificant
		Administrative Constraints Considered
		Environmental Factors Considered
		Systematic Weighing of Costs and Benefits
		Appropriate Leadership Style
		Organizational Attitudes toward Risk-Time-People-Work Considered
		Avoidance of Premature Positions
		Undue Defensiveness

TABLE 3.2. – (CONTINUED)

Management System: _____

Inappropriate Decision: _____

OK	Check Out	RESOURCE ADEQUACY
		Information
		Accurate
		Current
		Best Source
		Appropriate Comparisons
		Full Disclosure of Absolute Values
		Full Coverage (Current and Expected)
		Environmental Factors
		Administrative Constraints
		Resource Capabilities
		Critical Success Factors
		Cost-Benefit
		For Interest Groups
		Of Activity Itself
		Of Product-Service Outputs
		Upon Organizational Resources
		Cutoff Points
		Explicit Planning Premises
		Decision Makers
		Decision within Range of Competence
		Appropriate Consultation with Those Affected
		Healthy Attitude toward Environment
		Healthy Attitude toward Change
		Healthy Attitude toward Strategic, Long-Term Planning
		Conflicting Values
		Conflicting Attitudes toward Risk-Time-People-Work
		Respectful Attitude toward Specialists, Professionals, Skills Other Than Own
		Respectful Attitude toward Authority
		Appropriate Mesh of Age and Decision Complexity
		Time
		Sufficient Time
		Financial
		Support Level

TABLE 3.2. — (CONTINUED)

Management System: _____

Inappropriate Decision: _____

OK	Check Out	DECISIONS AND INFLUENCES
		Prior Decisions Imposed by Others or Self
		Objectives — Needs To Be Met
		Owners
		Consumers
		Suppliers
		Community
		Employees
		External Strategies — Ways To Accomplish Objectives
		Owners
		Consumers
		Suppliers
		Community
		Employees
		Internal Strategies — Ways To Carry On The Business Functions
		Production
		Marketing
		Logistics
		R & D
		Resource Acquisition
		Resource Maintenance & Development
		Employee Reward System
		Resource Compensation
		Resource Retirement
		Organization Structure
		Resource Allocations
		Authority Delegations
		Work Assignments
		Work Standards
		Work Evaluations
		Procedural Decisions, Self-Imposed
		Extraorganizational Influences
		Personal Goals
		Informal Group Pressures
		Peer Group Political Alliances
		Hierarchical Group Political Alliances
		Personal Obligations

Cooper, Arnold. "Identifying, Appraising and Reacting to Major Technological Change." Proceedings of the Winter Conference of the American Marketing Association, December, 1967.

Dory, John P., and Lord, Robert J. "Does TF (Technological Forecasting) Really Work?" *Harvard Business Review,* Nov.-Dec., 1970, pp. 16 ff.

Drotning, John. "Sensitivity Training Doesn't Work Magic." *Management of Personnel Quarterly,* Summer, 1968, pp. 14–20.

Ference, Thomas P. "Organizational Communications Systems and the Decision Process." *Management Science,* October, 1970, pp. B83–96. (The author proposes that more weight is given to information if the source was used more often in the past, if the source has a high position in the organization, and if the source is inside rather than outside the organization. With respect to the altering of information, the author proposes that favorable information is altered less than unfavorable data; the later the information enters the decision process, the less will it be altered; and, in ill-defined problems, information received through informal channels is preferred.)

Glueck, William F. *Business Policy—Strategy Formation and Management Action.* 2d ed. New York: McGraw-Hill, 1976. Pp. 60–61.

Guth, William D., and Tagiuri, Renato. "Personal Values and Corporate Strategy." *Harvard Business Review,* Sept.-Oct., 1965, pp. 123–32.

Howard, Jane. *Please Touch—A Guided Tour of the Human Potential Movement.* New York: McGraw-Hill, 1970.

Lawrence, Paul R., and Seiler, John A. *Organizational Behavior and Administration—Cases, Concepts, and Research Findings.* Rev. ed. Homewood, Ill.: Richard D. Irwin and The Dorsey Press, 1965. Pp. 602–9.

McDonough, Adrian M. *Information Economics and Management Systems.* New York: McGraw-Hill, 1963. P. 87.

Mintzberg, Henry. "A New Look at the Chief Executive's Job." *Organizational Dynamics,* Winter, 1973. Reprinted in *Business Policy—Strategy Formation and Management Action,* ed. William F. Glueck, 2d ed. New York: McGraw-Hill, 1976. Pp. 36–44.

Paine, Frank T. "Management Perspective: Sensitivity Training:

The Current State of the Question." *Academy of Management Journal*, Sept., 1965, pp. 228–32.

Schein, Edgar H., and Bennis, Warren G. *Personal and Organizational Change through Group Methods: The Laboratory Approach.* New York: John Wiley & Sons, 1965.

Taylor, Ronald. "Age and Experience as Determinants of Managerial Information Processing and Decision-Making Performance." *Academy of Management Journal*, March, 1975, pp. 74–81.

Vancil, Richard. "The Accuracy of Long-Range Planning." *Harvard Business Review*, Sept.-Oct., 1960, pp. 98–101.

Zani, William M. "Blueprint for MIS." *Harvard Business Review*, Nov.-Dec., 1970, pp. 95–100. (The key to a well-designed information system is in understanding the decisions to be made. These, in turn, define the kinds of information required.)

SUGGESTED READINGS

Ansoff, Igor H. *Corporate Strategy.* New York: McGraw-Hill, 1968.

Archer, Stephen H. "The Structure of Management Decision Theory." *Journal of Academy of Management*, Dec., 1964, pp. 269–87.

Brown, Rex V. "Do Managers Find Decision Theory Useful?" *Harvard Business Review*, May-June, 1970, pp. 78–89.

Drucker, Peter F. "The Effective Decision," *Harvard Business Review*, Jan.-Feb., 1967, pp. 92–98.

Gilmore, Frank F. "Formulating Strategy in Smaller Companies." *Harvard Business Review*, May-June, 1971, pp. 71–81.

Hammond, John S., III. "Better Decisions with Preference Theory." *Harvard Business Review*, Nov.-Dec., 1967, pp. 123–41.

Jones, Curtis H. "Applied Math for the Production Manager." *Harvard Business Review*, Sept.-Oct., 1966, pp. 20 ff.

McKenney, James L., and Keen, Peter G. W. "How Managers' Minds Work." *Harvard Business Review*, May-June, 1974, pp. 79–90.

Miller, David W., and Starr, Martin K. *The Structure of Human Decisions.* Englewood Cliffs, N.J.: Prentice-Hall, 1967.

Saunders, Charles B. "What Should We Know about Strategy

Formulation?" Academy of Management Proceedings, Annual Meeting, Boston, August, 1973.

Smalter, D. J., and Ruggles, R. L., Jr. "Six Business Lessons from the Pentagon." *Harvard Business Review,* March-April, 1966, pp. 64–75.

Zaleznik, Abraham. "Power and Politics in Organizational Life." *Harvard Business Review,* May-June, 1970, pp. 47–60.

4

Problem Finding, Before the Fact

Introduction

Up to now the problem finder has been engaged in gathering historical data in order to determine the basic causes for performance deviations. Only in rare instances is that kind of analysis really unnecessary. It is quite impossible to avoid all performance deviations. Nevertheless, there is ample room for improvement. A significant part of unsatisfactory performance would never have arisen if management had the capabilities, the inclination, or the time to spend on anticipating unsatisfactory performance.

Anticipations deal with expected future events. Problem finding, before the fact, is concerned with identifying deficiencies before operating performance deviations appear. This is forward-looking management and, by the way, the most difficult to perform effectively. The pressures of current problems, the lack of time, reward systems that pay out for immediate, short-run results, or the personal disinclinations of managers to deal with future problems militate against problem finding before the fact. Despite these formidable obstacles, there remain those who gain the advantage by doing their homework and those who have the capacity and inclination for this enriching approach to organizational management.

Before-the-fact analysis involves a change audit, a decision audit, an implementation audit, a resource audit, and an activity audit. In all instances, deficiencies attributable to those areas, by definition, will not as yet have produced unsatisfactory results; therefore, such deficiencies will not have been discovered in after-the-fact analysis.

A Reorientation—The Change Audit

The perspective of problem finding, before the fact, is different from that of problem finding, after the fact. While the initial focus in after-the-fact problem finding is directed to results, the before-the-fact problem-finding focus is on the environment, on decisions, on resources, and on activities, in order to detect elements that in the future may cause unsatisfactory results.[1]

The first question that is suggested in a change audit is

1. PFBTF assumes that all causes of past performance deviations have already been exposed. PFBTF, therefore, is a residual approach—its aim is to detect potential causes of possible future performance deficiencies.

this: Are the current sets of decisions still appropriate? "Still appropriate?" suggests that a number of things may have occurred or will occur to invalidate otherwise viable decisions:

- The relevant environment may have changed significantly.
- Organizational resources may have changed significantly.
- Organizational activities may have changed significantly.
- Decisions relative to the above have *not* changed.
- Other decisions have changed but the impact of such change upon those who will be affected has not been considered.

Changes in the Environment

Significant changes in the firm's external situation that are relevant to its survival or success require appropriate responses. For example:

- A decline in the supply of a major raw material
- Formation of a professional employees' union
- Changes in the work ethic
- Introduction of a new product by competitors
- Entry of a competing firm
- Highway relocation
- An increase in the demand for the firm's product

When these or other changes occur without the knowledge of an organization or are ignored, severe inroads into profits, sales, morale, or market position may occur. Problem finding, before the fact, suggests that environmental surveillance should alert decision makers to relevant and significant changes and energize decision makers to take appropriate steps to forestall performance deficiencies that will otherwise occur.

Changes in Organizational Resource Capabilities

Changes in the organization's capacity to respond to environmental circumstances are equally as important as knowing what changes in the environment are occurring or will occur. Effective strategy is based on an appropriate interface between environmental opportunities, obstacles, or constraints, on the one hand, and resource capabilities, on the other hand. Significant changes in resource capabilities may create a serious imbalance in the equation. This, then, may call for some change in strategy. For example:

- A decline in working capital
- An increase in productive capacity
- Equipment and technological obsolescence
- Management and professional obsolescence
- An increase in debt-equity ratio
- A large block of debt obligations maturing
- A decline in plant or store location

These and other considerations, as far as problem finding, before the fact, is concerned, stress the critical nature of change and the fact that awareness must precede an attempt to react.

Changes in Organizational Activities

Change in the nature of an organization's activities also may have an important bearing on the continued viability of "old ways" of doing things.

For example:

- An increase in the professionalization of line activities—this may call for a change in motivation and leadership techniques.
- Addition of new activities, such as research, advertising, public relations, engineering, or accounting, which may formerly have been contracted.
- An increase in the size and scope of activity—this may lead to greater complexity which, in turn, may call for structural changes.

Changes in Decisions

A change in policy or procedure, or almost any change in what, how, when, or why things are done, may create active or subtle resistance despite the best of intentions and sophisticated planning devices. The change audit relating to decisions can be facilitated when the problem finder has developed an awareness of the reactions of employees to these types of changes.

For many decades, social scientists have studied and experimented in the "change" phenomena in organizational life. The existence of resistance is indisputable. Just why it seems to arise in some cases and not in others, or why the resistance may at times vary inversely to the magnitude of change, is not quite so evident, and the suggested paths to avoid, diminish, or overcome resistance are controversial and diverse (Dalton, Lawrence, and Greiner). The common dimension for most of the suggested avenues for managing change deals with involving those who will be affected by the change. It would seem that, as a general guide, the ideas expressed in chapter 2 concerning leadership styles and the situational factors that determine appropriateness would also provide guidance here. The point is that the situation is the prime controlling factor for determining the degree of involvement of those affected by the change. This means that the problem finder in a before-the-fact situation should carefully diagnose the circumstances of the change in order to alert management if resistance may be expected due to the nature of the circumstances, the manner in which the change was decided upon, or the way in which it was introduced.

Decisions as the Focal Point

Problem finding, before the fact, is concerned with, not only the identification of change, but also its application; that is, its relevance with respect to decisions currently in force. The critical issue here is the impact of change upon established ways of doing things. The net result of this analysis is that potentially faulty decisions must be isolated before they produce significant deviations.

The Time-Lag Factor

The fact that changes in environmental factors, organizational resource capabilities, organizational activities, or decisions usually do not have immediate impact upon results provides management with the necessary lead time to adjust, react, or somehow compensate for change. Consumer preferences usually change rather slowly, competitive practices generally require time to become effective, and new technology may require years to gain full acceptance. All change, however, does not reflect such a tolerance level. Reaction time as a whole appears to be narrowing, while change itself appears to be increasing at an ever increasing rate. However, the existence of time-lag, whether long or short, does justify the process of problem finding before the fact. It also underlies the decision audit, implementation audit, resource audit, and activity audit.

The Decision Audit

Problem finding, before the fact, can also avoid possible future performance deviations by focusing on the consistency of current decisions with respect to the environment, with respect to each other, with respect to resource capabilities, or with respect to organizational activities.

Consistency with Environmental Circumstances

Perhaps one of the most serious deficiencies of decisions may be an inappropriate response or simply a lack of response to environmental circumstances. The immediate consequence of such lapses is only "work-in-process"; i.e., the effects will not be realized until some later date. The decision audit phase of problem finding, before the fact, attempts to uncover such inconsistencies before adverse results occur. The check of environment and decisions is, in essence, a review of past decisions where the environment has not appreciably changed. The problem finder asks, Did we make the right decision?

Consistency with Other Decisions

Decisions must be internally consistent with respect to each other so that activities governed by such decisions push or pull in the same direction. The question that must be asked is whether the directions established by prior decisions have been honored by subsequent decisions:

- Are strategies consistent with objectives?
- Is the organization structure consistent with product-market-technology choices?
- Are resource allocations consistent with priorities?
- Are strategies consistent with the simultaneous achievement or progress toward achievement of designated states?
- Are procedures and methods consistent with internal strategies (e.g., hiring procedures with personnel acquisition strategy)?
- Are work assignments and authority delegations consistent with personnel development strategy?
- Are work standards consistent with the achievement of various states (e.g., short- and long-run targets or countertargets)?

Consistency with Resource Capabilities

The third area of consistency deals with decisions and corporate resource capabilities. This could raise some of the following issues:

- Are motivation policies consistent with the needs, abilities, beliefs, or values of employees?
- Are decisions to expand or change product line overextending present resources or those expected during the planning horizon?
- Are decisions to adopt new technologies appropriate to financial and physical limitations?

Consistency with Organizational Activities

The fourth area of consistency relates to decisions and organizational line and resource activities. Some of the following concerns may arise here.

- Are compensation policies consistent with the nature of marketing activities?

- Are yardsticks and work standards compatible with the nature of the work performed?
- Are work assignments consistent with the overall tasks to be performed?

Internal decision inconsistencies, whether with respect to other decisions, resources, or activities, require change or amendments to the offending decisions. The point here is that the offending decisions must be explicitly identified. This then provides the focus for problem solving to commence.

Implementation Audit

An audit with respect to implementation concerns itself with the completeness of the implementation and with the nature and adequacy of communications with respect to implementing decisions.

Implementation—Completeness

An inadequate implementation readily brings performance failures. Some of the following areas may be investigated.

- Have required resources been planned for and budget allocations provided?
- Have actual work assignments and authority delegations been made?
- Have work standards been provided?
- Have structural implications been checked?
- Are new procedures or methods required, and if so, have they been developed?
- Have schedules been determined?
- Have work loads been determined?
- Have necessary functional strategies or policies been formulated?
- Have required training sessions been planned?
- Have periodic evaluations been planned?

Implementation—Communications

Decisions are necessary but not sufficient for success. Decisions must be communicated and be understood. This may raise some of the following concerns:

- Have decisions been communicated to all who will be involved or affected?
- Have any checks been made to ensure that decisions have been completely understood?

When a breakdown in implementation is found, it is important that the cause for such deficiencies be analyzed. The appropriate management system must be checked out. Problem-finding, after-the-fact, methods should be used when such a breakdown is discovered.

Resource Audit

Problem finding, before the fact, can also turn its attention directly to resources by inquiring into the continued adequacy and timely provision of resources to carry on current programs. Potential inadequacies may have been picked up during a change analysis or decision audit, but the aspect that may be overlooked relates to current resource inadequacies that have not as yet been felt in the results stage. The cause for such inadequacies may then be determined through problem-finding, after-the-fact, procedures.

Activity Audit

An activity audit is the final checkpoint in problem finding, before the fact. It attempts to determine if activities are being conducted according to plan. In effect, it becomes a check to determine whether or not "the way things are done" meshes with "the way things are supposed to be done." Laxity in supervision or inappropriate leadership styles may be found. For example, the price-fixing and bribery scandals of the sixties and seventies might have been identified much earlier under scheduled activity audits. The causes for any inappropriate conduct can be analyzed under problem-finding, after-the-fact, methods.

Summary

Problem finding, before the fact, attempts to avoid future significant deviations by—
- Recognizing significant and relevant changes in environmental factors, resource capabilities, organization line and staff activities, identifying changes in decisions themselves, and isolating the decisions that appear to be potentially ineffective in view of these changes
- Auditing current decisions for their consistency with the environment, with one another, with resource capabilities, or with organizational activities
- Checking out the adequacy of implementation decisions
- Auditing resources to check for the continued flow of required resources
- Auditing activities to check if conduct conforms to stated policy

The causes for decision inconsistencies, deficiencies in implementation decisions, resource flow, or in activity must be determined before problem solving can commence, since identifying inappropriate decisions and ultimately identifying defects in the decision-making system itself is needed to complete the problem-finding package. Table 4.1 highlights these steps and serves as a checklist. Columns are provided for indicating approval ("OK") or disapproval ("Check Out").

Data Sheets for Change Analysis

Sheets for recording data relevant to changes occurring or expected to occur in the environment, in resource capabilities, or in organization activities have been prepared to serve as checklists and as data banks.

The Data Sheet for Environment Change—Before the Fact (Table 4.2), provides an initial column for environment categories. These categories are similar to those listed in the Data Sheet for an After-the-Fact Environment Profile (Table 2.10). Column 2 provides for the measures to

TABLE 4.1.   STEPS IN THE PROCESS OF PROBLEM
FINDING, BEFORE THE FACT

OK	Check Out	
CHANGE AUDIT		
		Significant Change in Environmental Factors What decisions affected?
		Significant Change in Resource Capabilities What decisions affected?
		Significant Change in Activities What decisions affected?
		Change in Decisions Is the way in which the change was determined and applied appropriate to the situation?
DECISION AUDIT		
		Consistency With the environment With one another With resource capabilities With activities
IMPLEMENTATION AUDIT		
		Completeness What decisions need attention?
		Communication What decisions have not been communicated? Are decisions understood?
RESOURCE AUDIT		
		Continued Flow of Required Resources What resources are unavailable?
ACTIVITY AUDIT		
		Conformity to Policy What activities conflict with policy?

be used in describing the specific environment variables. The third column records changes occurring or expected for the short run and the long run. Entries listing long-run changes should also indicate, if possible, the expected rate of the change and its probability. These become the basic environmental planning premises. Column 4 interprets the change in terms of the premised impact upon the company. The impact is classified as an opportunity, threat, or obstacle-constraint. The premised impact should be stated in terms of consequences if no new actions are taken. The final column identifies the decisions that are affected by the change.

The Data Sheet for Resource Capabilities Change—Before the Fact (Table 4.3), has a similar format, except that the perceived impact of a resource change is classified in terms of a strength or a weakness.

The Data Sheet for Activity Change—Before the Fact (Table 4.4), has columns for recording the type of activity, its specific aspects, change occurring or expected for both the short run and the long run, and the decisions affected by the change.

Review of Problem-Finding Models

The problem-finding steps described in chapters 2, 3, and 4 are diagramed in Table 4.5.

Systems 1 through 3 relate to problem finding; systems A, B, and C are problem solving. The latter systems will be discussed in chapter 5.

References and Suggested Readings

REFERENCES

Dalton, Gene W., Lawrence, Paul R., and Greiner, Larry E. *Organizational Change and Development*. Homewood, Ill.: Richard D. Irwin and The Dorsey Press, 1970.

SUGGESTED READINGS

Bartlett, Alton C., and Kayper, Thomas A. *Changing Organizational Behavior*. Englewood Cliffs, N.J.: Prentice-Hall, 1973.

TABLE 4.2. DATA SHEET FOR ENVIRONMENT CHANGE – BEFORE THE FACT

(1)	(2) Measure or	(3) Change Occurring or Expected		(4) Premised Impact upon Organization[2]			(5) Decisions Affected
Category	Characteristic	Short Run	Long Run[1]	Opportunity	Threat	Obstacle-Constraint	by the Change

[1] Indicate the expected rate of change and the expected probability of change, if possible.
[2] For threat or constraint, indicate impact if no action taken; under opportunity, indicate potential opportunity.

165

166

TABLE 4.3. DATA SHEET FOR RESOURCE CAPABILITIES CHANGE — BEFORE THE FACT

(1) Category	(2) Measure	(3) Change Occurring or Expected		(4) Premised Impact upon Organization[2]		(5) Decisions Affected by the Change
		Short Run	Long Run[1]	Strength	Weakness	

[1] Indicate the expected rate of change and the expected probability of change, if possible.

[2] For a strength, indicate impact if no action taken to utilize; for a weakness, list consequences if no remedial action taken.

TABLE 4.4. DATA SHEET FOR ACTIVITY CHANGE – BEFORE THE FACT

(1)	(2)	(3) Change Occurring or Expected		(4)
Type of Activity	Specific Aspects	Short Run	Long Run[1]	Decisions Affected by the Change

[1] Indicate the expected rate of change and the expected probability of change, if possible.

167

TABLE 4.5.   REVIEW OF PROBLEM FINDING MODELS

SYSTEM 1   (PFATF Operations Analysis)

Activity	Problem finding, after significant deviations have occurred
Output	Causes of significant deviations: decisions or possibly some environmental factors

SYSTEM A   (PS)

Activity	Problem solving (decision making)
Output	Decisions to correct significant deviations

SYSTEM 2   (PFATF Management Analysis)

Activity	Problem finding, after management has produced inappropriate decisions
Output	Cause for the inappropriate decisions — i.e., some decision-making system deficiencies

SYSTEM B   (PS)

Activity	Problem solving (decision making)
Output	Decisions to correct decision-making system deficiencies

SYSTEM 3   (PFBTF Change audit, decision audit, implementation audit, resource audit, activity audit)

Activity	Problem finding, before significant operating deficiencies occur
Output	Potentially inappropriate decisions — i.e., decisions inconsistent with changes in the environment, with changes in resource capabilities, with changes in organizational activities, or with changes in decisions; failure to provide a complete set of implementing decisions; breakdown in the flow of resources; activities that conflict with policy; decisions currently inconsistent with respect to the current market situation, with other decisions, with current resources or activities

SYSTEM C   (PS)

Activity	Problem solving (decision making)
Output	Decisions to avoid future significant deviations

168

Dalton, Gene W. "Criteria for Planning Organizational Change." In *Organizational Behavior and Administration,* Rev. ed., ed. Paul R. Lawrence and John A. Seiler. Homewood, Ill.: Richard D. Irwin and The Dorsey Press, 1965. Pp. 914–27.

Greiner, Larry E. "Patterns of Organization Change." *Harvard Business Review,* May-June, 1967, pp. 119–28.

Irwin, Patrick H., and Langham, Frank W., Jr. "The Change Seekers." *Harvard Business Review,* Jan.-Feb., 1966, pp. 81–92.

Levinson, Harry. "Appraisal of What Performance." *Harvard Business Review,* July-Aug., 1976, pp. 30 ff.

Lippitt, Gordon L. *Organization Renewal.* New York: Appleton-Century-Crofts, 1969.

5

Problem Solving

Introduction

Problem solving embraces a process in which an attempt is made to find a course of action that will erase the significant deviations in performance. It also applies to situations in

171

which opportunities or threats arise and action is called for to meet those new developments. A survey of recent corporate records of U.S. businesses illustrates the kinds of actions taken in response to a poor showing or to new developments in the environment.[1]

- Acquired additional operating space
- Invested $1 million in additional production capacity
- Integrated separate product lines
- Accelerated expansion of retail operations
- Consummated sale of book division
- Instituted corporate-wide contingency program to effect cost savings
- Closed plant facilities in California and Kansas
- Introduced full warranty program
- Began national consumer advertising program

Generally, the efficacy of such actions is determined in large part by the diligence exercised in identifying the causes of past performance deficiencies and the degree to which the organization is aware of the opportunities and threats with which it is faced.

The problem-finding techniques developed in the preceding chapters will have identified some or perhaps all of the following kinds of problems that become the catalyst for problem solving:

- After the fact
  inappropriate decisions
  deficiencies in the management system itself
- Before the fact
  potentially inappropriate decisions due to changes in the environment, in resource capabilities, in corporate activities, or in decisions themselves
  inconsistent decisions and their causes
  implementation deficiencies and their causes
  causes of inconsistencies between behavior and policy
  causes of deficiencies in resource flow

---

1. Extracted from corporate annual reports.

Using such data, the problem solver should compile a composite resumé that briefly describes the full problem spectrum to be confronted. Additional backup data may also be noted —for example, identifying the significant deviations that resulted from the inappropriate decision. The problems should also have been arranged to reflect interdependencies. With such a resumé in hand, the problem solver may begin work.

Problem-Solving Methodology

The problem-solving sequence is the converse of the problem-finding, after-the-fact, sequence. Problem finding began with results and attempted to uncover inappropriate decisions. Problem solving begins with alternative courses of action, attempts to anticipate their effect, and chooses the action that best meets the criteria.

Specifically, the problem-solving sequence involves ten essential steps:

1. Develop *alternative* courses of action.
2. Identify the *environmental* variables that are relevant and significant for each alternative.
3. Identify the relevant and significant resource needs associated with each alternative; identify the current and expected future *organization's resource capabilities* profile with respect to each alternative.
4. Identify the relevant and significant *managerial decision variables* that may impinge upon each alternative.
5. Identify the relevant and significant *personal variables* that may affect the potential effectiveness of each alternative.
6. Find the *costs and benefits* associated with each alternative.
7. Determine whether or not each alternative *meets the minimum value* established for environmental, resource, managerial, and personal variables.
8. *Compare* alternatives against the criteria, and *choose* a course of action.

9. Decide upon appropriate *implementing actions.*
10. *Evaluate results.*

Problem-Solving Variables
(Optional Background Reading)

The ten-step approach to problem solving can be seen as a process of collecting, measuring, and analyzing information about a series of interacting variables.

Steps 2 through 5 are concerned with the collection of the data about those variables that will determine the nature of results; these are the independent variables. Step 6 is concerned with the collection of data about expected results— i.e., the expected values of dependent variables. Steps 7 through 9 are concerned with the analysis of the data and with a choice among alternative courses of action.

The problems about which the problem solver is concerned thus can be viewed as embracing a series of independent and dependent variables, represented by the systems design shown in Fig. 5.1.

The first three areas in the figure—environment, resources, and administrative (decisions)—can be broadly construed as the independent or causal forces; they are called variables because their value, force, or capabilities vary over time and among organizations. The latter three areas—action-interaction, output, and effects—represent the consequences of those prior forces; they are called dependent variables because their values are dependent upon the previous causal independent variables.

These two basic types of variables may be further analyzed as illustrated in Fig. 5.2.

Environmental variables may be seen as *antecedent* independent variables (AIV) because they represent a prior force. For example, a product need, whether active or latent, must exist in the market before sales can be made. The resources of the organization are the critical *intervening* independent vari-

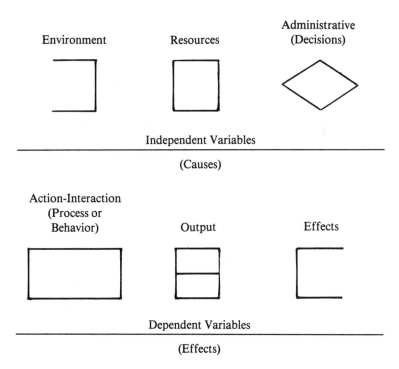

FIG. 5.1.   VARIABLES IN PROBLEM SOLVING

able (IIV) because they represent an intervening force between decisions and their effects. Such intervening resources
include employees, materials, and equipment. Decisions of
management, or the influences that ultimately run the organization, are the primary *independent* variables (PIV). They
represent the catalyst—e.g., a decision to provide some service or produce some product. All three are referred to as independent variables, although they will usually influence each
other as well as be influenced by the effects that they produce.
So, for example, a product strategy (PIV) is a function of
both the environmental variables (AIV) and the resource
variables (IIV); a motivation program (PIV) should be de-

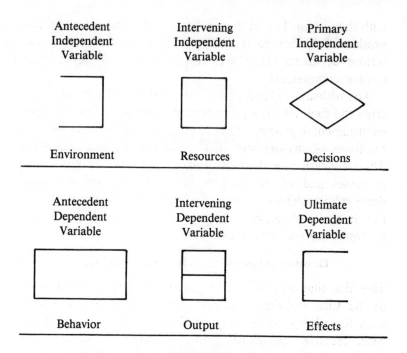

FIG. 5.2.   SEQUENCES OF VARIABLES

signed with the employee in mind (IIV). The results and effects of the program provide the feedback, which then may influence a change in the motivation program (PIV).

The dependent variables, which reflect the effects of the independent variables, include, first of all, the *antecedent* dependent variable (ADV)—i.e., the behaviors, the reactions, or the activities that occur by virtue of the decisions of management (PIV) and the properties, dispositions, or capabilities of the resources (IIV). It is considered antecedent because its operation is a necessary condition for the ensuing outputs to occur.

Output is the *intervening* dependent variable (IDV)—intervening between activity-behavior and the effects associated with the output. For example, the manufacturing process may produce defective parts (IDV), which in turn may cause serious accidents (UDV) to the purchaser of the malfunctioning components.

The *ultimate* dependent variable (UDV), therefore, represents the final effects of organization output or activity upon environmental groups. This dependent variable has become the focus of environmentalists, consumerists, and naturalists. Their concern is with the ultimate effects of the production processes and of the outputs of goods and services upon those who purchase or use the goods and services or who live in the environment that has been changed as a result of organizational processes.

Develop Alternative Solutions—Step One

The idea that at least two or three alternatives ought to be in the final running is more often ignored than followed, even though lip service may be given to the principle. Likewise, creative approaches may be solicited and even acclaimed as "our way" of doing things, but unfortunately, such approaches are often abandoned as disillusionment sets in. Something new for the sake of newness may have been the catalyst for attempting creative thinking. The "creative" alternatives may have been unrealistic in terms of saleability or corporate capabilities. Some feel that a stepwise approach to change tends to meet with greater success (Glueck), although major departures may be more appropriate in some cases. Major changes, however, imply greater complexity, greater evaluative sophistication, and more-involved implementing activities, and they may meet with stiffer resistance from those who must carry out the changes.

The development of alternative solutions is placed first on the problem-solving agenda in order to avoid the restrictive influence upon creativity that a formalization of restraints would otherwise impose. Under this arrangement, some exciting approaches may be discovered that otherwise might not have been found. Constraints that might otherwise have been perceived as insurmountable—thereby reducing the range of alternatives—may now be perceived as obstacles that can be overcome, albeit at some cost. For example, a budget limitation structures the thinking process to those alternatives that would not exceed the budgeted amount. In the absence of this restriction, all manner of possible action can be recommended for consideration. One such alternative might return benefits far in excess of the added risk and interest cost incurred by a higher initial capital outlay.

The process of developing alternatives obviously will not be conducted in a vacuum. Problem-finding sessions will have dealt at length with environmental, resource, managerial, and extraorganizational influences at work in the organization. The point is that the disciplined formalization of constraints in problem solving could well await the development of alternatives.

Table 5.1 is a sample work sheet for listing the alternatives for each problem area. Column 1 identifies the problem

TABLE 5.1.   WORK SHEET FOR LISTING PROBLEM
AREAS AND ALTERNATIVES

(1) PROBLEM AREA	(2) DESCRIPTION OF ALTERNATIVES

area that calls for a new course of action. Column 2 identifies and describes the alternatives that have been proposed.

Conducting Problem-Solving Sessions

The manner in which problem-solving sessions are conducted may be a critical variable for effectiveness. The type of problem situation is the key to selecting a procedure; some general guides for determining the most appropriate style may be found in chapter 2 under leadership styles. When a group approach appears most appropriate, interacting group processes have demonstrated their effectiveness. The interacting group—in contrast to the nominal group recommended for some problem-finding situations in chapter 2—relies for effectiveness upon active verbal interaction among group members. The stimulus and creativity arise from the ideas, responses, and reactions of group members to each other's contributions. Delbecq and others, in defense of interacting group processes, feel that the positive features of the social dynamics created by problem solving in group settings outweigh the negative aspects, particularly since groups can be structured to minimize the inhibiting influences that tend to occur and reduce group effectiveness (Van de Ven).

Identify Environmental Variables—Step Two

Step two deals with the identification of those relevant, but significant, variables in the environment that would affect the success of the alternatives under consideration. Some of the environmental categories were listed in chapter 2—for example, the nature of the resource supply market, and others. Obviously, all will not be relevant or significant, and the environmental profile may vary for each alternative.

Within each environmental category there exist perspectives, characteristics, or measures that reflect various dimensions of a given category. For example, competition may involve *size* of competitors, *number* of competitors, the *de-*

gree of competition, the *areas of cooperation,* the *norms* characterizing relationships, or the *means used to compete* (price, service, delivery, innovation). Some factor may be more important for one alternative than for another. Some could be irrelevant or have only insignificant effects upon the outcome of a possible course of action. Significance and relevance can also change with the passage of time.

After the relevant environmental dimensions have been identified, they should be assigned some value, if feasible. For example, *"Ten* competitors are expected to be active," or *"A 5 to 8 percent rate* of inflation is anticipated." These, then, become the planning assumptions.

The profile should preferably include expected environmental values over the planning horizon—i.e., the length of time required to recoup the investment, or the expected life of a product.

Greater sophistication is possible when probabilities are attached to values assigned to environmental forces. This means that a range of expected values is to be determined. For example, "We expect a 5 percent inflation rate with a 75 percent probability; or a 10 percent rate with a 25 percent probability."

The translation of environmental variables into their impact upon the alternative is the next step. Impacts may be classified in terms of opportunities, constraints, obstacles, or threats to the success of a proposed course of action. A given environmental occurrence may be considered as a threat by some firms but as an opportunity by others. For example, the advent of solid-state TV was seen as a serious threat by those firms that had entered the industry at a late date and had invested heavily in the manufacture of tube sets. On the other hand, this event was probably viewed as an opportunity by those whose investment had already been largely recovered.

A distinguishing feature among constraints, obstacles, and threats is that constraints are considered as that which cannot be overcome. The organization must simply carry on under the constraint. Obstacles, however, are events that can be circumvented but at some cost. Threats are *potential* constraints or obstacles that may or may not materialize. Some may see an event as a constraint, while others see it only as an obstacle. Some react prematurely or overreact to threats, while others seem to possess the capability, skill, and judgment to know when and how to react. For example, a new union can be seen as a constraint upon the exercise of corporate discretion. The union could, however, also be viewed as a temporary obstacle or perhaps as an opportunity. Automation, for example, could reduce labor content and overcome high wages. Or the contractual nature of work relations could provide the basis for dealing with labor problems on a prearranged and agreed-upon basis. Arbitrary action may be avoided by both parties to the contract.

Determining the impact upon the organization is not an easy assignment. It may require open and participative discussions by all affected by a given alternative. The impact issue can be demonstrated as follows: "Given a 9-percent inflation rate for the coming year, what impact can be expected upon the alternative of immediately replacing our milling machines?" Such answers as this would be reasonable: "The cost of borrowing money to purchase the machines will rise during the third quarter," or "We can expect to save 8 percent of the price of the machine if we purchase immediately rather than wait another year."

The work sheet shown in Table 5.2 provides the format for noting these dimensions of environmental variables. The environmental category and its measure are to be noted in columns 1 and 2. Current and future short-run values and future long-run expected values, with their respective probabilities, are noted in column 3. The last column provides space for classifying the variables and noting their perceived impact upon the success of a given alternative.

TABLE 5.2. ENVIRONMENTAL VARIABLES

(1) Category	(2) Measure or Characteristic	(3) Value						(4) Perceived Impact upon Alternative			
		Current	Future Short Run		Future Long Run			Opportunity	Constraint	Obstacle	Threat
			Value	Probability	Value	Probability					
EXAMPLE:											
Ecomonic Conditions	Inflation Rate	6%	5% 10%	.75 .25	8% 10%	.66 .33		**Short Run** Fully allocated cost of goods will be 5 to 10 percent below competition		**Long Run** In 5 years must replace equipment and lose cost advantage	

182

Identify Resource Needs and
Capabilities Profile—Step Three

Step three requires that, for each alternative, all significant resource needs be recognized. This means an answer to such questions as these:

- What are the crucial activities associated with success for this option?
- What resources are needed to carry on these crucial activities?
- What other resources are critical?
- When are the resources needed? This implies that immediate requirements are to be distinguished from those that can be phased in at some later time.

In addition, a resource capabilities profile must be constructed so that the feasibility of an alternative can be determined. Capabilities should be inventoried in terms of a current profile and an expected profile over the planning period. The expected profile will reflect resources that can be acquired, as well as the ability of the organization to acquire them at the proper time.

In order that the organization can capitalize on its strengths, both the present and future profiles should distinguish organizational resources on the basis of whether they represent strengths or weaknesses with respect to a given alternative. Recall that resources include the physical assets and the financial, human, technological, and informational resources. These would also embrace such things as location, dealers, and product line, and such intangibles as product reputation, for example. In defining critical activities, consideration should be given to both the technical business functions and the managerial functions. The definition of critical activities will then allow the determination of required resources for carrying on these activities.

Table 5.3 is a work sheet that illustrates the informational

TABLE 5.3. RESOURCE NEEDS AND CAPABILITIES PROFILE

(1) Needs		(2) Capabilities						
		Current			Future			
Critical Activities	Critical Resources	Strengths	Weaknesses	Impact upon Alternative	Strengths	Weaknesses	Impact upon Alternative
EXAMPLE:							
Manufacturing assembly	Experienced technicians		50% are inexperienced	This means supervisor's span of control must not exceed ten	Technicians will have been trained by company supervisors		Positive
Management quality control	Supervisors	90% are experienced and capable	With a reduced span would lack four experienced supervisors	Cuts production by 20% for the first year		20% to retire within 3 years	Negative, unless develop replacements

requirements for step three. The "needs" column provides space to record the critical activities and critical resource needs. The "Capabilities" column separates the current and future profiles, which in turn provide subcolumns for strengths, weaknesses, and their impact upon the alternative.

Some Observations about Resource Capabilities

There is a tendency for an organization to put too great a reliance on resources whose chief virtue is past accomplishment. Some guidelines are proposed below to alert the problem solver to this and similar kinds of resource fallacies:

- Avoid an overreliance on the results of past performance —for example, current share of market, loyal customers, or brand image. Such results should be seen in terms of the tangible capabilities that produced such results—for example, a quality product.

- One of the most important ways of distinguishing a product line as a strength or weakness is its stage of maturity in the product life cycle (Levitt; Dhalla).

- Decisions of management should not be considered as a resource strength or weakness. For example, it is fallacious to identify pricing policy as the primary strength that enabled the organization to achieve its predominant position in the market, if the intent is to consider pricing policy as a resource strength. Relying on past decisions can be disastrous for the organization. Price, after all, is a function of internal and external circumstances. Effectiveness in decision making should be seen in terms of the managerial talents that produced such decisions.

- Size of organization may be considered a resource; it is tangible in nature. However, whether it should be considered a strength or weakness depends on the situation. For example, the economies of scale are not infinite. On the other hand, smallness has its advantages in its increased flexibility to move quickly without the restrictive influence of tradition or of large fixed investments in plant and equipment.

Identify Managerial Decision Variables—Step Four

Decisions cannot be properly evaluated without reference to organizational purposes, objectives, or other pertinent decisions. Rarely can an alternative be formulated into action without reference to preceding decisions or traditions—that is, without considering the administrative decision variables. These are the constraints under which the problem solver must work. In effect they define the area of freedom in order that contradictory, inconsistent, or opposing courses of actions may be avoided.

Two areas of managerial decision variables should be made explicit by the problem solver. The first relates to previous decisions that have relevance and significance. They will usually include objectives, states to be achieved, the priorities among states, corporate traditions (the firm's way of doing things, which may not have been codified), previous decisions that may serve as precedents, and specific decision-making procedures that a particular group may have developed and codified.

The second area of managerial decision variables comprises those unique problem-solving decisions that are specifically constructed for the problem under consideration. For example, a specified support level, return-on-investment or profit-margin cutoff points, specific community regulations that must be observed, and the like. These become a part of the criteria that must be met. If not, the alternative must be discarded.

Table 5.4 illustrates a work sheet that may be used for noting these managerial decision variables. Columns are provided for the standing administrative decision variables and for the special problem-solving decision variables. Each is paired with a column for noting its impact upon the alternative under consideration.

TABLE 5.4. ADMINISTRATIVE DECISION VARIABLES

DECISION VARIABLES		DECISION VARIABLES	
Standing Administrative	Impact upon Alternative	Special Problem Solving	Impact upon Alternative

Identify Personal Variables—Step Five

The problem solver should next attempt to identify the significant and relevant personal variables that will be operating in a given problem-solving situation. This step is necessary so that the problem solver may be in a position to anticipate the nature of the resistance or cooperation that can be expected with respect to each alternative course of action. Reactions can arise in the decision-making process itself, in the managerial implementation process, or in the actual operation of carrying out the plan of action. These are the extraorganizational influences, the personal dimensions that have as their primary aim the welfare of entities other than the organization.

The extraorganizational forces may arise from individuals or from informal small groups within the organization. These forces can be identified in such terms as goals, norms, values, beliefs, attitudes, needs, or desires of those individuals or groups. They manifest themselves in efforts to form political alliances, the repayment of favors, the protection or the seeking of power positions, the building of empires, the ignoring of threatening information, or similar such behaviors.

At times inappropriate decisions can only be understood in terms of the decision maker's attitudes toward people, time, work, or risk, or in terms of his or her beliefs concerning certain cause-effect relationships. Identifying key values to which decision makers may tenaciously adhere can also assist in understanding why certain decisions were made. Such values may reflect high religious concerns or social concerns. They may reflect a high priority for economic or theoretical values. Aesthetic or political concerns may also be involved. Guth and Tagiuri relate that it appears that few decision makers are really aware of their value hierarchy (Guth and Tagiuri). It may be that associates can identify such values more accurately than the decision makers themselves. The point is that an awareness of these potential forces may aid in finding an alternative that will tap more of the positive forces of cooperation and less of the resisting forces.

A work sheet may be used to record the relevant and significant personal variables that will be active in a problem-solving situation. Table 5.5 shows a sample work sheet that is divided into the personal variables of decision makers and the personnel variables of operations personnel—i.e., the rank and file who will be doing the work. The decision-maker variables are listed in the left column, operating personnel variables at the right. Each main column has subcolumns for listing specific variables and showing their expected impact upon the success of the alternative under consideration. An example is provided on the work sheet.

Determine Costs and Benefits—Step Six

Determining the costs and benefits for each alternative can be a very tiring and involved process, yet perhaps no other step has more serious implications. Costs and benefits will almost universally be a characteristic of any action. Costs and benefits may also be thought of in terms of advantages and disadvantages or as implications and consequences.

It is helpful to view cost-benefit data from a number of perspectives in order that a complete spectrum of implications and consequences can be considered—for example:

- As a flow of costs and benefits throughout the period of time represented by the planning horizon—i.e., the useful life of a course of action or the time needed to recoup the investment.
- In terms of the interest groups that will be affected. These interest groups would include the organization, owners, the customers or recipients of organization products or services, the employees, suppliers, or the community.
- In terms of the broader human implications and consequences. The perspective here would relate to the psychological, sociological, political, or ecological impact of an alternative.
- From a systems perspective, namely:

TABLE 5.5. PERSONAL VARIABLES

TYPE	THE DECISION MAKERS (Individuals or informal groups)		OPERATIONS PERSONNEL (Individuals or informal groups)	
	Description	Impact upon Alternative	Description	Impact upon Alternative
Needs or Desires Goals or Aims Values Beliefs Attitudes Others				
EXAMPLE:				
Beliefs	Threats lead to improved productivity.	This would eliminate the alternative, since it is based upon the idea that, by granting more authority to a technician, improved motivation and performance will result – the carrot approach.	The people who do the work know best when to begin and stop the operation.	Meshes with the proposed alternative.

(This alternative recommended greater delegation of authority to computer technicians.)

input costs—e.g., capital funds and working capital required for resources; discretionary expenditures for overcoming environmental obstacles or for overcoming an alternative's dysfunctional effects upon organizational resources or upon environmental interest groups (e.g., antipollution devices, safety equipment, employee retraining, and the like).

activity costs—i.e., direct and indirect costs of operations. Economists would suggest using marginal or incremental costs in order to determine the true added cost of a contemplated course of action.

output costs—i.e., many adverse effects upon organization resources (employees, equipment, land, other programs or products of the company).

output benefits—i.e., profit, personal growth of employees, employment of community resources, increased tax base for the community, and the like.

• By the varying but specified conditions under which costs and benefits are expected to materialize—i.e., under various values of environmental variables, under various managerial support levels, or under various implementation methods (e.g., buy-versus-make decisions, decisions to overcome obstacles or the dysfunctional aspects).

The probabilities that have been attached to expected environmental events can now be combined to arrive at expected costs or benefits. These results can now be compared to the expected costs and benefits associated with other alternatives.

Viewing alternatives from several cost-benefit perspectives leads to several advantages. One is to produce an evaluation that should bear up under a wide range of interest-group and functionally oriented scrutinies. It should further provide a capability for demonstrating the effects upon expected results if planning assumptions do not materialize (sensitivity analysis). The procedure should also enable planners to determine the economies of phasing in resources when needed and to compare the values of flows of expected benefits over the lives of various alternatives.

The sample Implications and Consequences work sheet (Table 5.6) incorporates these cost-benefit ideas. Space is provided for inserting several conditions under which costs and benefits are expected to materialize. The conditions include the value of environmental variables, the support level, specified implementing actions, and the planning time period. Space is provided for benefits, for costs, and for cost-benefit outcomes (e.g., profit, present value of profit flow, ROI, or break-even point). The work sheet also provides for distinguishing costs and benefits by interest groups: organization, owners, customers, employees, suppliers, or community. Note that cost information can be distinguished as resource outlays, activity costs, output costs, or discretionary costs. Examples are inserted on the sample work sheet.

Measure Interface with Cutoff Points—Step Seven

Step seven requires that each alternative be compared against the minimum requirements for acceptance. These are the absolute managerial cutoff points that have previously been set up. If the consequences or implications fail to meet these basic requirements, the alternative is eliminated from further contention. The screening process may be carried on throughout the problem-solving process. This would eliminate the necessity of gathering complete cost-benefit data for alternatives that are obvious candidates for elimination.

These absolute prerequisites may include some of the critical environmental forces (e.g., government requirements), critical resource needs (e.g., line of credit), managerial cutoff points (e.g., ROI, profit, time), and critical extraorganizational constraints (e.g., norms).

Table 5.7 provides the format for noting the cutoff categories, measures, and minimum interface values; the alternative interface values; and eliminations. Interface values should be shown for each set of conditions; for example, Alternative

TABLE 5.6. IMPLICATIONS AND CONSEQUENCES

Alternative: Example: New Product A

Conditions: (a range of environmental or decision variables values may be tested)

Example:

Expected Value of Environmental Variables: Material cost increase 2% per year with a 70% probability

Support Level Decision Variable: Maximum (see schedule X for example)

Other Specified Implementing Decision Variables: Make own component parts

Planning Time Period: 5 years

Interest Groups	Benefits — Advantages — Implications	Costs — Disadvantages — Implications	Cost-Benefit Outcomes
Organization	**Example:** Volume _____, by year Income $_____, by year Plant utilization rate, _____ by year	Resource: Materials $_____ by year Activity: Labor $_____ by year Output: _____ Discretionary: By item $_____	Profit $_____, by year ROI _____, by year
Customers			
Owners			
Employees			
Suppliers			
Community			

1–Set A, 1–Set B; Alternative 2–Set A, 2–Set B, and so on. An example is provided on the sample work sheet.

Compare and Choose a Course of Action—Step Eight

Step eight manipulates, sorts, ranks, and analyzes the data accumulated during the previous steps and ultimately leads to a choice that best fits the multiple criteria. The criteria will involve the following facets of the situation:

- Environmental opportunities, obstacles, constraints, threats
- Resource needs versus resource capabilities
- Prior decisions of management
- Personal variables

Since in step seven the alternatives were screened to ensure that all alternatives for consideration met the minimum prerequisites for acceptance, it now becomes a matter of observing the degree to which each alternative meshes with the criteria. Problem-solving sessions now become involved affairs as diverse perspectives and dimensions call for simultaneous consideration. Unfortunately, a common measure for multiple criteria usually does not exist for these situations. It is here that the process may break down, and authoritarian dictates or personal preferences may become the escape routes for avoiding analytic and well-reasoned processes.

Establish Priorities

Simultaneous evaluation usually becomes an impossible task in complex situations, but an orderly evaluation can still be achieved by translating the criteria as well as the expected results of a contemplated course of action into the states they serve or will affect, and by retrieving or establishing priorities among the states that are involved in the evaluation. Recall that problem solving has up to this point:

- Developed data about relevant and significant environmental, resource, decision, and personal factors
- Screened alternatives against cutoff points

- Calculated cost-benefit data for each alternative under various condition sets:

  for various values of environmental variables

  for various resource support levels

  for various implementation methods—i.e., the discretionary cost factors or any unique implementation plan that could, for example, involve the production of needed parts rather than their purchase, or upgrading employees rather than hiring new employees

A priority list can be established by ranking the states from most to least important. A weighting factor could be added or the states may simply be grouped into classes—e.g., crucial, important, and marginal. When all relevant interest group concerns are represented by the chosen states, an integrated priority list becomes a reality.

Such an integrated priority list may be illustrated by the following example. Assume that an organization finds itself with a product line that is well into the maturity phase of its life cycle, and the organization diagnoses its chief problem in terms of its limited product line. The criteria that are being used must now be translated into the states that they represent. For example, government product regulations may be translated into "product quality"; consumer preferences, into "product acceptability"; corporate values to maintain a strong posture of good citizenship with respect to production processes and product features, into "social responsibility"; a tight money market, into "liquidity"; and the like. Table 5.8 illustrates some selected states that could represent the criteria variables. They have also been classified into three priority groups.

Of the eight states, three are considered as critical—product growth potential, an innovative line, and acceptability to the customers. A secondary priority list includes profitability with respect to providing the means to increase dividends, an opportunity for personal growth and advancement for employees, and the capacity of the product to reflect

TABLE 5.7. INTERFACE WITH CUTOFF POINTS (EXAMPLE: CONDITION SET A)

(1) Cutoff Category	(2) Measure	(3) Minimum Interface Value	(4) Alternative Interface Value				(5) Eliminations
			Alternative 1	Alternative 2	Alternative 3	Alternative 4	
Environmental	**EXAMPLE:** Federal fire retardant specifications	Meet minimum specifications	Yes	exceeds	Yes	Yes	
Resource	Cost of new equipment	$500,000	None	$400,000	$300,000	$500,000	
Administrative	ROI	10%	8%	10%	15%	12%	Alt. 1 (8%)
Extra-organizational							

TABLE 5.8.   SOME STATES REPRESENTING CRITERIA
VARIABLES

Criteria Variables		
CRUCIAL	IMPORTANT	MARGINAL VALUE
Growth	Profitability	
Innovation	Employee Growth	Uniformity
Acceptability	Social Responsibility	Quality

socially acceptable corporate behavior. A tertiary priority list identifies product uniformity and quality as marginal values.

Table 5.9 provides an example of some expected values for each of the eight states listed above, for three alternatives, under a given Condition Set A.

Consider Significant Costs-Benefits

An integrated priority list may not include some significant cost-benefits that were provided in the cost-benefit study. Such an omission tends to arise as a result of the semi-independent sources of criteria variables and the cost-benefit study. When problem solvers review both the criteria list and the cost-benefit data, they are provided with added insurance that the search for significant implications and consequences has not been bridled, biased, or restricted by predetermined criteria variables. A recheck of the cost-benefit study should probably be made at this time, so that any additions to the priority list can be made, if that seems appropriate. For example, the analysis of cost and benefits with respect to a resource supplier could have uncovered the dilemma that Alternative 1 would have a serious impact upon the product line of a major supplier of parts for the organization. Such a development might jeopardize a continuation of a mutually profitable relationship. If an alternative source of supply were more expensive, that implication could be incorporated into the integrated priority list. Or, in another vein, a check of condition sets may disclose that some benefit data reflect

TABLE 5.9. INTEGRATED DECISION VARIABLE PRIORITY LIST WITH AFFIXED VALUES FOR ALTERNATIVES

Priority Group	State or Characteristic	Measure	Expected Value for Alternative		
			1-A	2-A	3-A
I Crucial	Product Growth	% annual increase over product life	Average of 10% over 6 years	Average of 15% over 4 years	Average of 20% over 3 years
	Product Acceptability	Units sold over life of product	40,000	45,000	15,000
	Innovative Nature of Product	Number of significant differences from competitors' products	1	3	1
II Important	Owner Profitability	Present value of marginal profit	$150,000	$140,000	$15,000

III Marginal	Employee Growth	% labor content represents skilled labor	50%	10%	30%
	Community Responsibility	Potential hazard to user	Disposal	Emission	None
	Product Uniformity	Variance from product operating specifications	± 10%	± 5%	± 10%
	Product Quality	Expected life of product without major repairs	2 years	1 year	5 years

rather low probabilities although the benefits themselves appear exceedingly attractive. In view of this, the problem solver may choose to add a risk factor to the priority list.

Some Other Considerations

Some other tasks and considerations may face the problem solvers before they are in a position to make a choice. For example:

- Confirm the accuracy of the cost-benefit data; data filtering could have hidden some important truths.
- Be aware of human hindrances to effective data evaluation.
- Remember, the more bureaucratic the organization, the more difficult it will usually be to affect a real change.
- Determine whether decision makers have a vested interest in the solution under consideration. If they do, the chances are that an objective evaluation will be more difficult.
- Resist the recurring temptation to "salvage" a previous inappropriate decision.
- Determine whether decision makers have retained conflicting perceptions of the situation facing an organization; if so, work to resolve them.
- Look for a hidden agenda that may move members of the problem-solving group into directions that can only be understood in terms of power, interpersonal relationships, and personal goals—the extraorganizational influences. Note that such influences may arise from those who will make the recommendation, those who must approve the choice, and those who must implement the choice.
- Also try to detect predetermined choices that were made some time before reaching this stage of the problem-solving process. Such choices reflect the inherent dislike for analytic processes characteristic of many decision makers.

Some Guides to Effective Choice

The following guides to effective choice may be useful:
- Attempt to capitalize on what the organization is capable of doing best.
- Attempt to "lead from corporate strengths."
- Remember that flexible plans are useful devices for dealing with future contingencies. The greater the constraints, however, the less the flexibility that is possible; but the greater the uncertainty, the greater the flexibility one will want.
- Consider implementation implications before making a firm choice.
- One of the most important criteria for choice must remain whether or not a course of action will change past or expected future unsatisfactory results.
- Note that the problem-solving process is itself a matter of a cost-benefit tradeoff; i.e., the cost in time and dollars expended should not exceed the expected benefits.
- Combining alternatives may be a viable choice pattern.

The Choice

The problem solver is now in a position for a final evaluation and choice. The final working papers from which a choice should emerge comprise a series of expected values for criteria variables associated with each condition set, for all alternatives. The gathering of data, preliminary screening, translation of criteria into states, and the determination of priorities have been achieved. The full spectrum of interest group concerns, environmental variables, corporate resource capabilities and requirements, administrative decision variables, and extraorganizational influences, translated into states where possible, has been considered and incorporated into the final working papers. The conditions under which expected costs and benefits will materialize have been made explicit. Probabilities should have been attached to planning

assumptions where feasible. Costs and benefits have been
adjusted by their associated probabilities. Discounted or
present values of costs and benefits should have been computed, where necessary or appropriate, in order that alternatives can be properly compared. The time for the exercise
of sound judgment has now arrived.

A final matrix of costs and benefits may appear in the
general format shown in Table 5.10.

TABLE 5.10. MATRIX OF COSTS AND BENEFITS

Priority Class	I			II			III		
Alternative Condition Set	States								
	a	b	c	d	e	f	g	h	i
1-A									
1-B									
2-A									
2-B									
3-A									
3-B									

Three alternatives, each under two condition sets, and corresponding values for nine states are represented by this
matrix. To the degree that the appropriate states are represented and the "other considerations" followed, the matrix
should provide the problem solver with the data with which
to make a reasonable choice.

The significance of the condition sets in deciding upon
an alternative is an important dimension of the evaluation
process.

● Results will vary with support level; the choice of a more
   desirable result must be tempered by the feasibility or
   desirability of the higher support costs.
● Results will vary under varying implementation methods;

the choice will rest upon results and the desirability or feasibility of a given implementation approach.

- Overall results will vary as the time horizon is extended; choice will depend upon organization needs and upon the inclination of decision makers as to the mix of short- and long-run results that is most desirable.

- Results will vary with expected values of environmental factors; probably the most significant factor that will influence choice is the degree of risk the organization wishes to absorb.

The final choice will now be determined by a combination of the rational and perhaps the irrational, the pressures inherent in the decision variable constraints, the demands of extraorganizational forces, the dominant managerial perception of the situational variables, the kind of support that management is willing to provide, the risks management is willing to absorb, and the confidence it puts in the data assembled. The choice will not be perfect, but the choice should be one in which considerable confidence can be placed.

The choice process, however, has only begun: the work done so far is the visible portion of the iceberg. Perhaps 90 percent of the action remains to be taken—i.e., the carrying out of the implementation process.

Decide upon Appropriate Implementing Actions —Step Nine

A review of the previous step will suggest some of the more critical implementation decisions that must still be formalized. These are briefly summarized below.

- Financial support to fund resource needs up to the support level, including the expenditures of discretionary costs and the other implementation actions upon which expected results were based

- Resource acquisition and development plans

- Activity support to fund the required operations to carry out the program

- Structural plans involving work assignments and authority delegations
- Control plans involving the establishment of standards against which results can be measured
- Motivational plans to secure the cooperation of those who must administer, supervise, and carry on the operations

Evaluate Results—Step Ten

The evaluation of results is the final step in the problem-solving process. To assume that the problem is solved after a decision has been implemented is, of course, nonsense; yet, this is too often the expectation of many organizations.

The evaluation should preferably be a continuous activity. The six-month or annual performance review is not a particularly effective approach, since it is based upon an after-the-fact situation. When an organization adopts a before-the-fact preventive approach, it should not revert to the formal annual or semiannual performance review as its primary vehicle for uncovering problems. Rather its primary reliance for review should be based upon a continuous flow of information concerning operations. Critical intermediate results areas may be established. The point is that management will want to be in a position to detect potential problems or deficiencies in the new course of action before serious deviations can result.

In the final chapter, a business organization will be analyzed from the perspective of the problem-finding, problem-solving methodology.

References and Suggested Readings

REFERENCES

Dhalla, Nariman F., and Yuspeh, Sonia. "Forget the Product Life Cycles." *Harvard Business Review,* Jan.-Feb., 1976, pp. 102–12.

Glueck, William F. *Business Policy—Strategy Formation and Management Action.* New York: McGraw-Hill Book Co., 1976. Pp. 118–19.

Guth, William D., and Taguiri, Renato. "Personal Values and Corporate Strategy." *Harvard Business Review,* Sept.-Oct., 1965, pp. 123–32.

Levitt, Theodore. "Exploit the Product Life Cycle." *Harvard Business Review,* Nov.-Dec., 1965, pp. 81–94.

Van de Ven, Andrew H. *Group Decision Making and Effectiveness.* Kent, Ohio: Kent State University Press, 1974, pp. 19–20.

SUGGESTED READINGS

Ackoff, Russell L. *A Concept of Corporate Planning.* New York: Wiley-Interscience, 1970.

————. *Scientific Method.* New York: John Wiley and Sons, 1962.

Beckett, John A. *Management Dynamics: The New Synthesis.* New York: McGraw-Hill Book Co., 1971.

Christensen, C. Roland, Andrews, Kenneth R., and Bower, Joseph L. *Business Policy—Text and Cases.* 3d ed. Homewood, Ill.: Richard D. Irwin, 1973.

Drucker, Peter F. *Management: Tasks, Responsibilities, Practices.* New York: Harper and Row, 1974.

Glueck, William F. *Business Policy: Strategy Formation and Management Action.* New York: McGraw-Hill Book Co., 1967.

Hicks, Herbert G., and Gullett, C. Ray. *The Management of Organizations.* New York: McGraw-Hill Book Co., 1976.

Koontz, Harold, and O'Donnell, J. *Management: A Systems and Contingency Analysis of Managerial Functions.* New York: McGraw-Hill Book Co., 1976.

Kotler, Philip. *Marketing Management—Analyses, Planning and Control.* Englewood Cliffs, N.J.: Prentice-Hall, 1972.

Luthans, Fred. *Introduction to Management: A Contingency Approach.* New York: McGraw-Hill Book Co., 1976.

Newman, William H., and Logan, James P. *Strategy, Policy, and Central Management.* 7th ed. Cincinnati: South-Western Publishing Co., 1976.

Optner, Stanford L. *Systems Analysis for Business and Industrial Problem Solving.* Englewood Cliffs, N.J.: Prentice-Hall, 1965.

Schnelle, Kenneth E. *Case Analysis and Business Problem Solving.* New York: McGraw-Hill Book Co., 1967.

Schoennauer, Alfred W. *The Formulation and Implementation of Corporate Objectives and Strategies.* Oxford, Ohio: The Planning Executives Institute, 1972.

Steiner, George A. *Top Management Planning.* Toronto: Collier-Macmillan Canada, 1969.

6
Problem Finding and Problem Solving, Organizational Analysis

Background

An actual company situation will be used in this final chapter to demonstrate the application and value of a systematic approach to organizational analysis. The circumstances of the case provide a greater opportunity to illustrate problem finding than problem solving. However, some of the pitfalls of premature solutions will be illustrated, and the data provided in the case should provide an interesting exercise for the creative reader.

The names and places have been disguised, but the setting is in one of the largest of Great Britain's Commonwealth nations during the seventies. British Apparel, Ltd., a subsidiary of British Consumer Industries, Ltd., of Great Britain, was experiencing symptoms of a company in deep distress but was separated by thousands of miles from its home office. The parent organization (BCI) dispatched an experienced manager from its headquarters in an effort to pull its fledgling back to profitability and long-term health. About six months after the arrival of John Eden, he had formulated a strategy for improving the performance of British Apparel, Ltd. However, prior to any major change, John Eden hired a consultant from the university to diagnose the organization and confirm his prognosis.

Dr. Arthur Henry was introduced to the management staff of British Apparel, Ltd., and given a tour of the plant. Mr. Eden carefully described to Dr. Henry the major problems as he perceived them and set out his proposed approach to alleviate the malfunctions. All employees had been apprised of Dr. Henry's role, and management personnel were directed to provide him with any information he might request. Office space was made available in the apparel display room. Space was at a premium at British Apparel, since it was experiencing increased demand for its products. Time was considered of the essence, and a report was expected within four weeks.

John Eden's Proposal

John Eden reviewed the British Apparel dilemma with Dr. Henry. He was frank and direct in his appraisal. His major points were these:

- Employee turnover was catastrophic.
- Costs of production were rising.

He saw an alleviation of these conditions in terms of:

- Greater participation by workers
- Greater opportunities to work in small groups

He further felt that the group approach required testing on a small scale before a full commitment could be made.

Dr. Henry was now on his own. He keenly felt his responsibility to his employer as well as to the employees who might be personally affected by his proposals. During the fact-finding stage, several employees provided unsolicited information and leads that they felt should be investigated. During the course of the analysis, it was learned that the future of some staff members had already been determined. In effect, plans had been drawn in final form for implementing directly or indirectly John Eden's ideas for greater participation, not only by workers, but among management personnel as well. Implied in John Eden's remarks had been that participation, consultation, and involvement had to be practiced at all levels of management if participative management at the supervisor-worker level was to be successful.

Where to Begin

Concepts

By using the problem-finding and problem-solving methodology as a framework, one can "get one's bearings" and determine what stage in the process one has entered. This becomes the first order of business in any problem situation. The second concern is to determine the unit of analysis that represents one's area of responsibility.

Fig. 6.1 may help the manager or consultant visualize the stage to which organizational analysis has already progressed and, therefore, delineate what remains to be done as his or her own area of responsibility. The four column headings identify the basic processes in organizational analysis and design:

- Problem finding, after the fact, operations analysis
- Problem finding, after the fact, management systems analysis
- Problem finding, before the fact
- Problem solving

The row headings identify the main purpose of each process and the subprocesses involved:

- AIB (actions-interactions-behaviors)
- R (resources)
- E (environment)
- D&I (decisions and influences)

Application

It was only fair to assume that John Eden had spent considerable time in surveying the situation, had arrived at what could be an accurate conclusion, and, as his plans were being finalized, had instituted a cross-check in the person of Dr. Arthur Henry.

If this assessment was correct, the consultant would be primarily concerned with reassessing the unsatisfactory performance and suggesting solutions. Yet Dr. Henry could sense the commitment John Eden had to his solution and that perhaps his true role was to implement that course of action. But, if British Apparel, Ltd. was in dire straits, then the situation would first call for problem finding, after the fact. Before-the-fact analysis and solution implementation must wait. Dr. Henry, therefore, chose to start at the very beginning of after-the-fact problem finding.

The Unit of Analysis

Concepts

By definition, the unit of analysis spells out the internal and external factors of a situation. If participants in a prob-

FIG. 6.1. THE PROBLEM-FINDING AND PROBLEM-SOLVING PROCESS

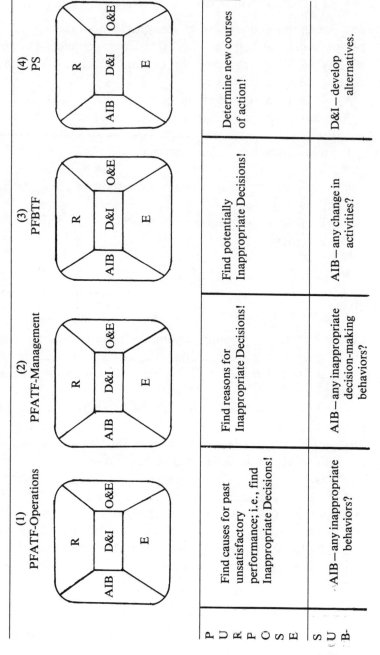

	(1) PFATF-Operations	(2) PFATF-Management	(3) PFBTF	(4) PS
P U R P O S E	Find causes for past unsatisfactory performance; i.e., find Inappropriate Decisions!	Find reasons for Inappropriate Decisions!	Find potentially Inappropriate Decisions!	Determine new courses of action!
S U B-	AIB—any inappropriate behaviors?	AIB—any inappropriate decision-making behaviors?	AIB—any change in activities?	D&I—develop alternatives.

PROCESSES

R – any resource deficiencies?	R – any resource deficiencies?	– are decisions consistent with activities?	R – identify environmental variables.
E – any unexpected conditions?	D&I – identify causal self-imposed decisions or influences!	– are behaviors consistent with decisions?	– determine resource needs and capacities.
D&I – what decisions inappropriate?	E – any causal decisions or influences imposed by superiors?	R – any change in resources?	– determine decision variables, including cutoff points.
		– are decisions consistent with resources?	– determine personal variables.
		– is resource flow adequate?	– find costs and benefits.
		E – any change in environment?	AIB – compare with cutoff points.
		– are decisions consistent with environment?	– compare alternatives.
		D&I – any change in decisions?	D&I – establish priorities.
		– are decisions consistent with other decisions?	AIB – make a choice.
			Implement.
			Evaluate.

continued

– are decisions fully
  implemented?

– are decisions
  adequately
  communicated?

Key:

PFATF   Problem finding, after the fact
PFBTF   Problem finding, before the fact
PS   Problem solving

AIB   Activities – Interactions – Behaviors, significant and relevant
R   Resources, significant and relevant
E   Environment, significant and relevant
D&I   Decisions and Influences
O&E   Output and Effects

lem situation have not agreed upon the unit of analysis, it becomes exceedingly difficult to discuss the issues. Participants may well contribute from perspectives irrelevant to the problem at hand.

Application

British Apparel manufactured and marketed its products domestically and on an international scale including the United States. It meticulously investigated competing products and was active in designing its own creative styles. It purchased its raw materials, hired its employees, and was able to manage itself as a semiautonomous unit. The chief exception to self-rule involved major expenditures, which required the approval of the home office.

The manufacturing operation was divided into five product lines, each of which was subdivided into four operations. The essential elements of the formal organization chart are shown in Fig. 6.2.

Since John Eden had directed the study toward production, it was chosen as the unit of analysis. This meant that the other departments—sales, purchasing, personnel, and accounting—would comprise the "external environment." Although requests for inputs from these departments would be a legitimate area of inquiry for Dr. Henry, their internal operations would be beyond his immediate area of interest.

After-the-Fact Problem Finding

Concepts

The purpose of PFATF is to determine causes for unsatisfactory performance. This means that the following actions must be taken:

- Get results data across a broad spectrum of the unit of analysis.
- Identify the target range.
- Determine if the targets were appropriate.
- Compare results and targets and determine where significant deviations exist.

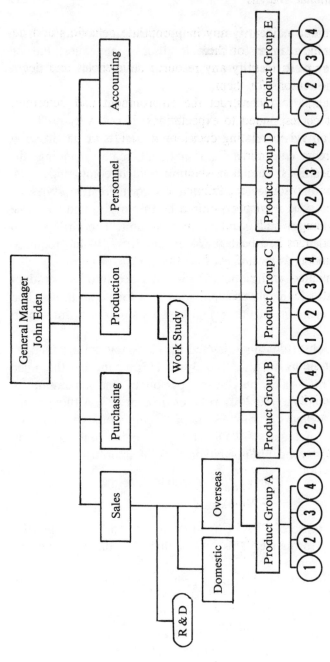

FIG. 6.2.   ORGANIZATION CHART, BRITISH APPAREL, LTD.

- Attempt to identify any inappropriate behaviors and determine reasons for them.
- Attempt to identify any resource deficiencies and determine reasons for them.
- Attempt to reconstruct the environment and determine if it corresponded to expectations; if not, why not?
- As an aid in relating decisions to results or to clues, inquire or determine:
  if decisions were consistent with each other, with company resource capabilities, with organization activities, or with environmental conditions.
  if changes had occurred in resources or activities or if changes had been made in decisions affecting the unit under review. If so, had they been adequately implemented and communicated to those who were to be affected by them?

Application

Data were requested about the following production department states:

STATES	MEASURES
• Productivity	• Output by department, by week
• Work quality	• Rejects by department, by week, as a percent of output
• Employee satisfaction	• Percent of absences by department, by week
	• Annual employee turnover by department
	• Number of complaints received so far this year (about four months) by department
	• Number of employee suggestions received so far this year (about four months) by department
	• Number of accidents so far this year (about four months) by department
	• Length of service by department

For the first two states, the data provided relevant measures with respect to the products produced; data for the third state served as indirect measures of employee job satisfaction. All the data received had been extracted from existing company records, but in most instances the information was supplied in the form in which it had been originally accumulated. This meant that payroll and production records had to be consulted, minutes of meetings read, and reference made to accounting records. The information apparently had never been subdivided according to product group. The data about rejects, quality, accidents, and employee suggestions were in a form that could not be subdivided at this late date.

Table 6.1 is a record of the performance of those subdivisions that failed to reach minimum targets on the four measures for which appropriate data by subdivision were available.

TABLE 6.1. RECORDS OF UNDERPERFORMING
SUBDIVISIONS

Unit	Output in % of weeks below target	Turnover % per year	% of employees 1 year service	% of all complaints received
A4	90	70	50	18
D3	80	110	20	15
B4	60	80	40	(8)
A1	60	(30)	(<10)	(0)
E3	50	80	70	(0)
D1	50	(30)	(<10)	(0)
E4	40	120	40	(8)
A3	30	100	40	(0)
D2	(10)	90	50	(7)
D4	(10)	90	30	13
A2	(0)	100	20	(0)
C4	(0)	50	30	(6)
E2	(0)	50	(<10)	12

( ) Within target range

Inappropriate Behaviors

Concepts

One of the first areas that could provide clues for unsatisfactory performance comprises past behaviors, interactions among resources, or activities. The activity-interaction-behavior area involves work flow, effort exerted, behavioral patterns, communication patterns, leadership style, supervision, and adherence to policy or work rules.

Application

Dr. Henry realized that time was of the essence under the charter granted to him by John Eden, and that to personally observe plant operations would be very time consuming and most likely rather unreliable. He had already sensed this; his presence on the premises had created no mild stir. In addition, unsolicited visitors to his office provided him with important leads, most of which were later confirmed. During several of these informal sessions and the periodic formal meetings with management and technical personnel, the following conditions were noted:

• Work flow: observations
—Interruptions in the production process had occurred at various times and in various locations due to lack of work at the job stations. Records were unavailable as to the duration of the interruptions or where they had occurred.

• Work flow: possible reasons
—The temporary work flow stoppages were apparently caused by scheduling and job order sequencing procedures that were inadequate for the present scale of operations.

• Leadership style: observations
—The style of management, including the supervisory level, could be generally described as autocratic and directive.

- Leadership style: possible reasons
  —The style appeared to be a reflection of the traditional approach to management for this organization.
  —The nature of the tasks could be generally described as:
    reasonably repetitive and routine, but disturbed by several product style changes during a normal work week
    easily learned (except in subdivision one)
    having limited promotional opportunities
    being of the nature that the operator possesses some control over work speed
    requiring a reasonable state of task attentiveness, but one that would not be unduly restrictive of social interactions
    reflecting a relatively high degree of job specialization based upon a well-established and slow-changing technology
    possessing very limited opportunities for creativity, except in work methods improvements
    being dependent upon the output of a preceding station in terms of on-time and uniform output
    requiring a standing position for most operations, and representing immediately measurable output

In light of this description, the task-oriented leadership style appeared to be reasonably appropriate and did not appear to be disruptive in achieving minimum production output targets.

- Communication patterns: observations
  —Based on a limited sample, it appeared that supervisors by and large initiated and controlled interactions with the workers.
  —This observation was reinforced by complaints that many girls would not approach their supervisors and by expressions that reflected the belief that some supervisors were unapproachable.
- Communication patterns: possible reasons
  —A directive leadership style with strong task orienta-

tion is often characterized by this kind of communication pattern. The factory council, which was a recent innovation, reinforced the pattern. Meetings were chaired by management, and discussion topics were limited to items of mutual interest.

- Behavioral patterns: observations
  —Several extreme types of employee behaviors were evident in the work situation. One subdivision indicated that operators held back discussing their grievances, several groups claimed blatant discrimination, while two groups asked for the ear of management personnel other than their immediate supervisors.
- Behavioral patterns: possible reasons
  —It appeared that supervisors in their quest for task achievement had failed in the human dimension of the task with respect to some of these operators.
  —Formal or informal training in human relations for new supervisors did not exist.

Resource Deficiencies

Concepts

The second clue area is concerned with identifying resource deficiencies that existed during the period under review. The ramifications of resource deficiencies could include:

- Amount
- Quality
- Specification match
- Time
- Place

Application

The following resource deficiencies were found in the production process:

- Shortage of qualified foremen: observation
  —Some vacancies for foremen existed. Openings were posted on company bulletin boards, but applicants

were few. Recently one foreman was transferred in from England.

- Shortage of qualified foremen: possible reasons
  —Foremen were paid on a straight salary basis and did not receive overtime pay. Workers had frequent opportunities to earn such pay. As a result, foremen often earned less than the workers they supervised.
- Labor supply: observations
  —Some subdivisions appeared to be understaffed.
- Labor shortage: possible reasons
  —Pay scale was average for similar work in the community, although the large mass-production firms were now offering higher wages and improved fringe benefits.
  —Opportunity for overtime at premium pay rates existed. Some operators felt overworked due to repeated requests to work late.
- Working conditions: observations
  —Plant facilities were overcrowded but relatively clean, some temperature extremes existed in winter and in summer, noise and fumes became irritants for some subdivisions, and eating areas were relatively small, as they had recently been reduced.
- Working conditions: possible reasons
  —The company had recently expanded its operations, due to increased demand for its products, and had reassigned some lunch room space to factory operations.

Environmental Conditions

Concepts

The conditions and circumstances in the relevant environment of an organization are major considerations in arriving at appropriate responses. In after-the-fact analysis, an attempt must be made to construct a profile of the environment as it actually existed during the period under review in order to identify clues for unsatisfactory performance.

Application

The following environmental conditions appeared as significant and relevant factors for understanding the problems facing the production department:

- All mass-production firms in the area faced a labor shortage. It was difficult to recruit young or middle-aged operators who would be willing to stay in a factory-type operation. A severe drop in immigrants dried up the potential labor pool. The first generation nationals by and large refused to consider factory employment as a permanent career opportunity.
- Government policy encouraged worker participation in decision making in both public and private corporations.
- Inflationary pressures were mounting throughout the country as well as worldwide.

The company reacted to these conditions by hiring more and more women and ordering considerable overtime production.

Decisions as Causes

Concepts

Problem finding, after the fact, is based on the premise that unsatisfactory performance is essentially caused by management fumbles. However, to establish a logical relationship between results and management decisions is a difficult task. The concept of independent and dependent variables is a useful mechanism for structuring the problem finders' thought processes. Here content knowledge—i.e., understanding the relationship between the nature of the situation and management methods—is all-important. Problem-finding methodology here cannot substitute for such content knowledge. Fruitful areas for investigation in identifying inappropriate decisions may include checking into the consistency of decisions, identifying changes in the system, and determining if decisions have been adequately implemented.

Application

Dr. Henry reviewed the operation in light of the ideas expressed in behavior analysis, resource analysis, and environmental analysis. The following decisions appeared to be deficient in the context of the significant deviations found in the production department:

- Promotion policy–salary policy
  —A policy to promote from within coupled with a pay differential for supervision became self-defeating as heavy overtime schedules placed some operator wages above those of the foremen.
- Qualifications of foremen
  —An emphasis on technical proficiency of foremen was not supported by foremen proficiencies for working through people to accomplish output targets.
- Work incentives, suggestion system, and methods improvement program
  —Work incentives were based upon output above a minimum base. The minimum reflected an output value that employees could easily attain. Trainees were paid the base rate until they had learned their job. If they failed to reach the minimum within a reasonable time, they were released.
  —A methods improvement scheme provided that, if an operator reported a methods improvement idea that he or she had originated, the operator would receive 50 percent of the first year's savings. The work study group or the supervisor was permitted to check the method used on any operation at any time in order to determine whether or not a change had been initiated by an operator. These policies appeared to be ineffective, as evidenced by sixteen formal work value

changes during a six-month period. All had been worker-induced, but fifteen had been identified by supervisors or the work study group, and only one had been reported by the employee through the suggestion scheme route.

One of the most amazing discoveries occurred when Dr. Henry computed the average outputs of the eight subdivisions that experienced weekly outputs below target. Using 100 as the index for on-target *average* performance during the most recent four-month period, the record appeared as shown in Table 6.2.

TABLE 6.2. OUTPUTS BY SUBDIVISION

Subdivision	Average Output Index	Percent of Weeks Output below Target
A4	95	90
D3	94	80
B4	100	60
A1	100	60
3	101	50
D1	100	50
E4	100	40
A3	103	30

Only the two poorest performers averaged output below 100; another was at 103; one was at 101; and four managed to achieve 100. This remarkable overall output record, which by and large came exceedingly close to the 100 index for all of the eight subdivisions, was attained despite the fact that output, when measured by the percent of weeks it fell below target, ranged from 30 to 90 percent. The probability that the output records could reach these averages due to random occurrences appeared to be exceedingly low. The only reasonable explanation was that the averages were "managed" by the groups themselves. Who stood to gain? The operators,

of course, since they were guaranteed the minimum base pay
irrespective of output; and for those weeks in which they produced above target, they would receive incentive pay. Who
stood to lose? The organization, of course. Although average
did reach target, the cost of that output was considerably
higher per unit than if the target had been consistently reached
every week. Although the stated purpose for methods improvement was cost reduction, the policies influencing production actually produced higher costs per unit.

- Qualification of foremen—nature of employees: Six of
  eight subdivisions whose output fell below target were
  staffed completely by women employees. Their turnover
  rate was 84 percent. Four additional subdivisions that
  employed only women averaged a 61 percent turnover
  rate. All-male departments averaged a 41 percent turnover rate. Of all employees, 63 percent were now women,
  and the percentage of females was rising. But the nature
  of supervision had not changed since the days when most
  employees were men. If the premise is accepted that supervisory styles should reflect a different mix under all-
  female conditions, then an apparent inconsistency is
  evident.

The resumé of after-the-fact problem finding shown in Fig.
6.3 illustrates a plausible set of interrelationships among the
component parts of the production system.

- The drop in output was caused by work-flow interruptions, which in turn were caused by poor task sequencing
  and task scheduling by management.
- The drop in output was aggravated, particularly if measured by cost per unit, by stockpiling or averaging arrangements of the work groups involved—the end product of their group norms. Group norms appeared to be
  reactions to management's work methods improvement
  program and the incentive pay scheme, coupled with
  the rather unsuccessful paid suggestion scheme.
- The drop in output may also have been affected by the

shortage of operators and foremen. Operator shortages were a product of the drop in immigration (the traditional source of many applicants), the attitude toward factory work of the first generation nationals, and the other opportunities available in a booming economy. Management reacted by authorizing massive overtime and by hiring more and more women operators. The higher overtime pay opportunities provided further incentive for the work groups to enforce their work norms; and the higher proportion of women in the work force further aggravated an already high turnover rate, since the rate for females was significantly higher than for their male counterparts.

- The high turnover rate was probably an important factor in the output drop. The turnover rate was also more significant for female than male operators. With this perspective, it appears that the high initiation and control of interaction by supervisors probably drew out the extremes in employee behavioral pattern. The pattern fits the triad of interpersonal responses developed by Horney, namely, move against, move toward, or move away (Horney). The practically exclusive technical orientation of supervisors (in the context of more and more women operators) was the mechanism that produced the irritant in terms of the one-sided communication pattern. The lack of any training device for inculcating the human dimension of the supervisor's work responsibilities was the reflected management deficiency.

After-the-Fact Management System Analysis

Concepts

The analysis of the management system is intended to identify elements that may have produced past inappropriate decisions. The chief parts of the investigation include the decision-making process; the resources that were used (infor-

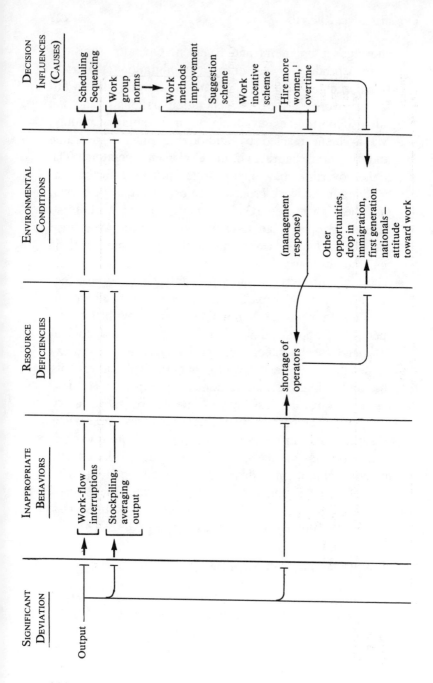

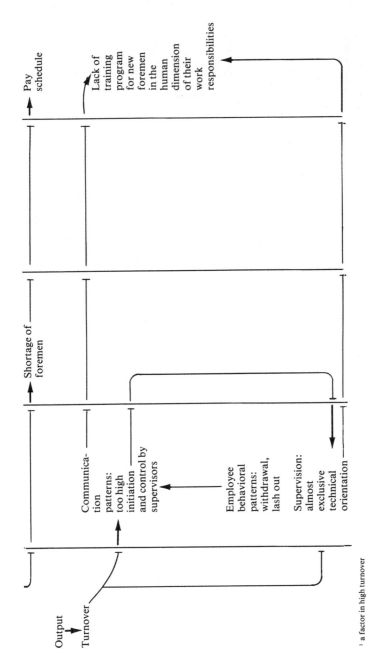

FIG. 6.3. RESUME OF AFTER-THE-FACT PROBLEM FINDING

[1] a factor in high turnover

mation and the decision makers, primarily); the decisions that were self-imposed to channel and direct the process, and those that may have been imposed by higher management. Included, of course, would be any extraorganizational influences that could be identified. The purpose of this exercise is to correct any deficiencies, if possible, in order to diminish the chances for a possible recurrence of ineffective decisions.

Application

An analysis of the decision-making system is difficult. Rarely does an outsider have the opportunity to observe the system in operation. The case of British Apparel, Ltd., was no exception. During the course of the investigation, however, several apparent deficiencies were identified.

- The decision-making process, according to well-informed sources, had been a one-man show. With increased demand, growth in the scope of operations, accelerated style changes, and foreign competition, one man did not have the time to keep abreast. The lack of sophistication in scheduling was a prime example. Work study was far behind in remeasuring job values for management-induced changes. The ramifications of growth had apparently escaped prior top management. Evidence was lacking that any meaningful evaluations had been conducted at the subdivision levels of product groups. Management's efforts seemed to have been largely devoted to dealing with external pressures. This meant that control of internal affairs inevitably suffered. The new head of British Apparel was committed as a matter of principle to decentralization in decision making. The deficiency had been recognized and a course of action chosen to correct the deficiency in the person of John Eden.

- The second major deficiency dealt with a lack of management-type information by which internal control could be accomplished. It was soon apparent that management was unaware of the degree to which subdivisions contributed to output deficiencies, and the rich storehouse of data remained unanalyzed by cost units. The deficiency in information had remained uncorrected.

Before-the-Fact Problem Finding

Concepts

The aim of before-the-fact problem finding is to identify any element that has not been identified in after-the-fact problem finding and may cause future unsatisfactory results unless some action is taken. The areas that could suggest a need for new action would include:

- Any changes in the environment, organization resource capabilities, activities, or decisions
- Inconsistencies between decisions on the one hand, and other decisions, resource capabilities, activities, or environment, on the other hand
- Deficiencies in implementing decisions
- Inconsistencies between behavior and policy
- Deficiencies in the continued flow of resources

Application

Dr. Henry's primary concern was with analyzing the unsatisfactory performance of the production department; however, John Eden had already begun to carry out his plan to delegate more authority to his middle management group and to require that they in turn decentralize their departments to a much greater degree than in the past. He was also a strong believer in group processes and insisted that group meetings be held at each level of management to discuss matters of mutual interest. Ultimately he hoped to bring participative management to the grass-roots level, but this had to await Dr. Henry's report.

While before-the-fact analysis was beyond the immediate scope of Dr. Henry's work, the need for this kind of thought process was forcibly called to management's attention. This event occurred during the initial supervisory training sessions, which, by the way, all management personnel attended. A training film on problem solving was used to introduce the new management philosophy. By the third session, it became apparent to management that, by and large, the managerial staff did not possess a workable grasp of the process and work of managers. In other words, an obvious inconsistency between the decentralization strategy and the present capabilities of the management staff had come to light. This would delay the implementation of the decentralization strategy.

Other inconsistencies also became apparent under the new management philosophy of John Eden. Complaints increased, and management responded by giving assurances that factory supervisors would be available to listen to "real" grievances. In addition, a factory council was inaugurated to discuss matters of "mutual interest." It would be chaired by management. In effect, management was saying that in the future the supervisor would have the time to listen to "real" complaints and that the employee could take an issue of "mutual interest" to the factory council through his factory representative.

These courses of action, however, appeared to be inconsistent with employee needs. Issues that would qualify to be heard were those seen as "real" or of "mutual interest." Unfortunately, however, experience suggests that most employees find it difficult to express to their supervisors or to other management staff the true reason for their discontent. They may couch their irritation in socially acceptable terms or (as in Mayo's experience) voice their complaints in a way that does not even provide a clue as to the real source of the dissatisfaction (Mayo). Exit interviews confirm this observation. Only employees who left during the most recent four months —8 percent of those who left—gave reasons that might be construed as directly critical of management policies.

The factory council decision also appeared to be inconsistent with the nature of the supervisors' work. Worker-supervisor relations were obviously at a low ebb. Employees found it difficult to talk with their supervisors. What was needed was a strengthening of the role of supervisors in terms of the human dimension. But asking workers to bring complaints to a factory council rather than to their supervisors would not encourage better supervisor-employee relationships. In fact, it might well discourage them altogether, considering the current state of those relationships.

The factory council decision, however, could conceivably have been interpreted as a necessary alternative in view of the present nature of employee-supervisory relations and, therefore, quite in accord with reality. This observation illustrates the idea that, throughout problem finding and problem solving, the impact of cause and effect is seldom absolute and varying interpretations are possible.

An important change had also occurred in the environment. The government had launched a program that put considerable pressure on private firms to move toward worker participation in management. Mandatory participatory provisions for the public sector were begun and position papers published urging the private sector to follow suit. John Eden's management philosophy meshed well with the government's position. The timing was phenomenal.

Resumé of Problem-Finding Conclusions

In after-the-fact problem finding, the following inappropriate decisions, decisions that could bear review, extraorganizational influences, and environmental obstacles were found:

- Schedules and work sequences
- Supervisor pay policy
- Work methods improvement program
  work methods suggestion scheme
  work incentive scheme
  work group norms

- Tight labor market
  overtime
  hiring more women
- Lack of foreman training in the human dimensions of their work responsibilities

The causes are sorted into five packages. All have been interpreted as being closely related to the production output deviations or high employee turnover for designated subdivisions of the production department. Scheduling is the most obvious deficiency. The other decisions have not produced the kind of results that management was seeking. These must be reviewed in order to determine what amendments, changes, or new approaches are feasible in order to deal with the key deviations—high unit costs of production and high turnover.

In after-the-fact management system analysis, the following deficiency that still required attention was noted:

- Lack of management-type control data

In before-the-fact problem finding, using as a time perspective John Eden's administration, the following elements were found that would probably lead to future significant deviations:

- Middle management and supervisors were essentially technical men rather than managers who could operate in a decentralized environment.
- Restricting discussions with supervisors and the factory council to "real" and "mutual interest" matters was inconsistent with the current response patterns of employees.
- The factory council decision was inconsistent with the role that supervisors were now expected to play.

Before-the-fact problem areas, in this example, were products of efforts made to correct past symptoms and to implement a new management philosophy. All probably required review. The implementation of the decentralization strategy had already been postponed, after the capabilities of the management personnel were realized. The other inconsistencies represent warning signals that suggest that the inconsistent decisions should be reevaluated.

Problem Solving

Concepts

Problem solving is concerned with correcting courses of action, or instigating new ones, for those decisions identified as probably inappropriate. Ultimately all opportunities, constraints, obstacles, threats, inappropriate behaviors, resource deficiencies, deficiencies in the management system, changes, inconsistencies, or implementation deficiencies must be perceived in terms of their common dimension: What course of action must be taken to deal with the situation of which they are a part? This is problem solving.

Most problem-solving situations require that each phase of the ten-step problem-solving sequence discussed in the previous chapter be considered in arriving at a choice. "Good" managers do these things without overt reference to a methodology, but internal or external pressures may result in shortcuts. An explicit methodology provides a convenient checklist and is of inestimable value as a training device.

Application

Nine problem areas were uncovered during the problem-finding phase:

- Work schedules and sequences
- Supervisory pay policy
- Determining a course of action for dealing with the tight labor market in which previous responses involved overtime and hiring more women
- The work methods improvement dilemma, which involved the methods improvement program, the paid suggestion system, and the work norms of some work groups
- The lack of human relations skills on the part of factory foremen
- The lack of management-type information
- The inconsistency of the new decentralization strategy with management capabilities
- The inconsistency of restricting employee-supervisor dia-

logue to "real" and "mutual interest" areas when viewed
in the context of the current state of employee-supervisor
relations
- The inconsistency of the factory council decision with
  the desired role of supervisors

Determining Which Problem Takes First Priority

Concepts

Nine problem areas face the organization. Where to begin
must be resolved with the situation in mind. Various criteria
are possible:
- Those that represent immediate problems or those that
  reflect long-range problems
- Those that represent basic decisions or those that reflect
  implementing decisions
- Those that represent crucial issues and those of less importance
- Those that represent issues to which top management
  gives top billing

Application

John Eden had fairly well established the priorities. In effect, he had said, "We must correct the production cost problem, and the implementation of decentralization throughout
the organization holds the key."

The high cost of production was a function of the failure
of some of the subdivisions to meet their minimum weekly
quotas. The most immediate event preceding the actual failure
to meet weekly quotas could be found in the activity-interaction cell (behavior). Correcting behaviors would have the
most immediate effect if this could be done with existing resources. The inappropriate behaviors were determined to be
the temporary no-work conditions on the factory floor and
the averaging and stockpiling behavior of some work groups.
The decisions or influences that acted upon those behaviors

were associated with an absence of sophisticated work schedules and work sequence procedures, plus the influence of work-group norms. The group norms were influenced by the work incentive scheme, the work methods improvement program, and the work improvement suggestion scheme. The above analysis suggested, therefore, that a reevaluation of work sequences, work schedules, and the entire incentive–work methods strategy would have the most immediate effects upon the cost of production.

Correcting deficiencies in resources would tend to have the next most immediate effect. Resource deficiencies existed in terms of shortages of foremen and operators. The foreman shortage appeared to have been associated with the salary policy, while operator shortages were associated with the complex environmental situation. The foreman shortage was not considered as crucial as the operator shortage, and therefore reviewing British Apparel's response to the operator shortage was considered as the next most important issue. This decision was prompted by the extremely high turnover of women employees, which had contributed to the high production costs.

The high female turnover rate was associated with complex behavioral patterns that seemed to run parallel to the extremely high task orientation of foremen. Associated with these supervisory deficiencies were the restrictions placed on topics for supervisor-employee dialogue and the structure of the factory council. These decisions were given a third priority rating and would be reconsidered in the context of correcting the behavioral deficiencies of supervisors and encouraging improved employee-supervisor communications.

Reconsideration of the supervisor salary policy was listed fourth; dealing with the inadequacy of management information for evaluating subdivisions was rated fifth; and implementing decentralization was placed last.

The low priority given to an information system could be questioned. The justification used was that more immediate problems crowded out this important control instrument.

The decentralization approach for solving British Apparel's problems, sought by John Eden, could not yet be implemented, as middle management and supervisory capabilities would not justify the change at this time. What had occurred here was a rather common phenomenon. The situation was expected to cope with a new management method—the very opposite of effective management, which carefully considers the situational factors before deciding on method.

Task forces were assigned to each problem area. The work schedules and sequences were contracted to a consulting firm. Other areas were assigned to internal task groups, but the decentralization issue was postponed until such time as management capabilities could be updated. Participative management at the grass-roots level could not be justified on technological grounds. It could only have been justified on account of political considerations.

References

Horney, Karen. *Our Inner Conflicts.* New York: W. W. Norton & Co. Pp. 48–95.

Mayo, Elton. *The Social Problems of an Industrial Civilization.* London: Routledge, 1949. Pp. 60–76.

Index

239